THE CHILDREN OF KAUAI

The Children
of Kauai

*A Longitudinal Study from
the Prenatal Period to Age Ten*

Emmy E. Werner, Jessie M. Bierman, and Fern E. French

HONOLULU
UNIVERSITY OF HAWAII PRESS
1971

Library of Congress Catalog Card Number 77-122904
Standard Book Number 87022-860-9
Copyright © 1971 by University of Hawaii Press
Manufactured in the United States of America

Contents

TABLES

Preface

THIS STUDY PRESENTS the results obtained during more than a decade of cooperation among the members of a multidisciplinary team representing maternal and child health, obstetrics, pediatrics, psychology, public health nursing, sociology, and statistics, and several thousand families of a multiracial community living on the island of Kauai, Hawaii. It began when Hawaii was still a territory and ended after the islands had become the 50th state of the Union.

Throughout this time, differences in professional orientation had to be bridged across more than 2,000 miles of Pacific Ocean which separated the research staff at the University of California from the field staff of the State of Hawaii Department of Health and the University of Hawaii.

The reader familiar with other longitudinal studies of human development will appreciate the administrative, technical, and financial problems involved in maintaining a study of several thousand mothers and their children over more than 10 years and in preserving, at the same time, a continuity of goals.

Our debt to all those who contributed to the study is inestimable. Angie Connor, M.D., M.P.H., acting executive officer of the Waimano Training School and Hospital, was codirector of the study and the pediatrician of the field staff. Louise P. Howe, Ph.D., research sociologist, was the resident director of the study during the early years and was primarily responsible for the planning and overseeing of the special examinations and interviews. Myrna Campbell, M.P.H., was supervisor of public health nursing in the Kauai district of the State of Hawaii Department of Health during the early years, and was field director of the ten-year follow-up. Ruth S. Smith, M.A., clinical psychologist, Kauai Mental Health Service, was responsible for the psychological examinations and the environmental ratings of the 10-year follow-up.

Our thanks also go to the practicing physicians of Kauai and the pediatricians and psychologists who conducted the follow-up examinations; the staff of public health nurses and social workers who conducted the family interviews; to Kenneth Simonian and Marilyn Vaage who were statisticians on the Berkeley staff; and to Marjorie P. Honzik, Ph.D., who contributed significantly to a number of publications and gave generously of her advice.

Financial support for the study came from the Children's Bureau (Research Grant PH 200); from the National Institute of Child Health and Human Development (Grant No. 7734); and from General Research Support (No. 1-S 01-FR-5441-04), University of California, Berkeley.

We express appreciation for permission to reprint excerpts from some of our publications to the American Academy of Pediatrics; the American Psychological Association; the American Public Health Association; the Society for Research in Child Development; the Journal Press, C. V. Mosby Company; and to the *Journal of Tropical Pediatrics and Child Health*.

Finally, our thanks go to the families of Kauai to whom this book is dedicated in the Hawaiian spirit of *Kokua* and *Aloha*—with good will and good wishes to the children of all races, East and West.

THE CHILDREN OF KAUAI

CHAPTER 1

Introduction

BEGINNING IN 1954, a team of pediatricians, psychologists, and public health workers from the University of California, the University of Hawaii, and the State of Hawaii Department of Health followed the course of over 3,000 pregnancies on the island of Kauai, and studied over 1,000 of the live-born children and their families for a full decade.

The purpose of the present report is to summarize and integrate the findings of this longitudinal study. We have described here in a concise way the course and outcome of the pregnancies and the way in which a cohort of the children had developed by the time they had reached the preschool and school years, and have added illustrative cases to show the short- and long-term influences of perinatal stress and quality of environment.

When this study began, one of its principal goals was to observe and document the course of all the pregnancies and their outcomes in an entire community, from the women's first missed menses until the children were 10 years old. In a natural history fashion, we reported *what* happened and *when*. We noted the fetal deaths from the earliest weeks of gestation as well as the deaths that occurred among the live-born infants and among the children. We learned as much about the type and severity of perinatal complications as we could. For the infants born alive, we noted their physical and mental defects and sought to associate these with significant events during the course of each pregnancy, labor, and delivery. Finally, we assessed the physical, cognitive, and social development of the children when they were two and 10 years of age. From the beginning of the study, we recorded information about the material, intellectual, and emotional aspects of the family environment into which the children were born and in which they grew up.

1

By obtaining a body of data over a period of time by careful observations of all pregnant women in an entire community and of the children they produced, we hoped to set in perspective the good outcomes as well as the poor ones and to get some idea of what the poor outcomes meant to the children, their families, and the community. This goal had not been served by the clinical literature which was based on restricted samples nor by the large number of short-time, intensive studies which had attempted to establish associations between single variables and various unfavorable outcomes.

Our first concern was to identify, as early as possible, each woman who had become pregnant and to obtain as much information as possible about the pregnancies, both those that ended in the loss of the conceptus and those that produced live-born children. But we soon broadened our interests to a consideration of environmental factors in the home and the community and the association of these factors with the development of the children.

With data available on the course and outcome of all pregnancies in an entire community comprising all socioeconomic and ethnic groups in the population, from four-weeks' gestation until the children were 10 years old, we were able to: (a) calculate the incidence of fetal and postnatal deaths and perinatal complications; (b) evaluate the associations between perinatal stress and the physical, cognitive, and social development of preschool and school-age children using the diagnostic tools of pediatrics, psychology, and allied disciplines; (c) assess the relative effects of perinatal stress and quality of environment (material well-being, intellectual stimulation, emotional support) on the development of the children at two and 10 years of age.

We believe that the findings from this longitudinal investigation are relevant to present and future health, educational, and social-action programs for children, especially the "culturally deprived," and that they will be of interest to concerned citizens as well as to students and professional people in the fields of child development, education, maternal and child health, obstetrics, pediatrics, psychology, and sociology.

In chapters 1–4, we describe the setting and the population of our study, and the ways in which we enlisted the cooperation of the families and the children. We briefly review related studies, contrast them with the design of the Kauai investigations, and delineate the procedures used for data collection in the prenatal period, labor and delivery, and in the follow-up phases at two and

10 years. We conclude this section with an assessment of the family environment.

Chapter 5 contains an account of the outcome of all pregnancies occurring in the community from early gestation to birth, the incidence of fetal and neonatal mortality, the type and severity of perinatal complications, and the congenital defects which were identified during the first two years of life.

In chapters 6 and 7, we show the short- and long-term effects of perinatal complications and environmental deprivation on the physical, cognitive, and social development of preschool and school-age children.

Selected cases, summarized in chapter 8, illustrate both "good" outcomes and "poor" outcomes—a variety of significant physical handicaps, learning disabilities, and behavior problems.

Chapter 9 deals with the predictive value of early pediatric and psychological examinations.

In chapter 10, we describe significant variations in child development associated with cultural factors. Contrasted here are the developmental patterns of Caucasian children with the Oriental and Polynesian children who constituted the majority of the study group.

In chapter 11, we report sex differences in the rate of intellectual maturation and responsiveness to achievement demands in the home.

The final chapter summarizes our major findings and their implications. The relevance of the data for planning programs of prevention, diagnosis, and rehabilitation, and the implications for professional education and services for children, is discussed.

A RÉSUMÉ OF LONGITUDINAL STUDIES

Longitudinal studies of normal child development, focusing on the cognitive development and socialization experiences of children, had their beginnings in the United States in the late 1920s and early 1930s. There are now 10 major longitudinal studies that have secured a large variety of measurements on samples of Caucasian, predominantly middle-class, children and have followed them from infancy for 10 years or more. Descriptions of their methods, goals, and findings have been summarized by Bloom (1964) and Kagan (1964).

The major studies that have relevance to the Kauai study are the Berkeley Growth Study and the Guidance Study of the University of California's Institute of Human Development; (Macfarlane

TABLE 1   Effects of Perinatal Complications in Early Childhood

Investigator	Age at Follow-up	Type of Impairment at Follow-up[a]				
		Neurological	Motor	Perceptual	Intelligence	Personality
Graham et al. (1957)	Neonatal	+	–	–	–	+
Prechtl (1960)	2–9 days	+	–	–	–	+
McGrade et al. (1965)	3–4 days	–	–	–	–	+
Honzik et al. (1965)	8 months	–	+	+	+	+
Stechler (1964)	10 weeks–25 months	–	+	+	+	–
MacKinney (1958)	36–42 months 6, 12, 18, 24 months, 36, 42, 48, 54, 60 months	–	–	–	0 +	–
Prechtl (1965)	2–4 years	+	–	–	0	+
Ucko	3, 6, 9, 12, 18 months 2, 3, 4, 5 years	–	–	–	+ 0	+
Graham et al. (1962)	3 years	+	–	0	+	+
Keith et al. (1953)	early childhood	0	–	–	0	–
Niswander et al. (1966)	4 years	–	0	0	0	0
Apgar et al. (1955)	5 years	–	–	–	0	–

NOTE: Reprinted, by permission of the American Academy of Pediatrics, from E. E. Werner, K. Simonian, J. M. Bierman, and F. E. French. 1967. Cumulative effect of perinatal complications and deprived environment on physical, intellectual, and social development. *Pediatrics* 39: 490–505.

[a]Presence of significant impairment reported by investigator is indicated by (+), absence by (0), and a dash indicates impairment not studied.

4

1938; Jones and Bayley 1941); the Fels Institute Study at Yellow Spring, Ohio (Sontag, Baker, and Nelson 1958; Kagan and Moss 1962); and two British longitudinal studies, one in London (Hindley 1961; Moore 1968) and one in Newcastle upon Tyne (Spence et al. 1954; Miller et al. 1960).

Longitudinal studies of events occurring during pregnancy and their associations with childhood disorders, such as mental retardation, cerebral palsy, speech and reading disorders, perceptual and behavioral problems, are of more recent origin. Most were initiated in the 1950s and 1960s. Exclusive of investigations limited to premature infants, nine studies have been reported in the English literature (both from the United States and Europe) that begin with documented birth histories and follow children with perinatal complications (using normal babies as controls) during the neonatal period, infancy, and the preschool years. Fourteen studies (again using normal children as controls) follow children with perinatal complications during their school years, at some time between five and 15. A summary of the major findings of these studies is presented in tables 1 and 2.

The investigators differed in their choice of criteria for the selection of their subjects and studied different functions. Children were selected because of a special perinatal complication or condition at birth (e.g., anoxia) or a particular place of birth (such as a teaching hospital). Only a few completed studies (Keith, Norval, and Hunt 1953; Graham, Caldwell, Ernhart, Pennoyer, and Hartman 1957; Keith and Gage 1960; Prechtl 1960, 1965; Perinatal Research Branch 1960–present; Graham et al. 1962) have followed children at more than one time in their lives in order to observe both short- and long-term associations between perinatal stress and later development.

The need for longitudinal studies of the effects of perinatal complications has been highlighted by Teuber and Rudel (1962), who presented evidence from studies of both children and adults with brain injuries that some behavioral manifestations increase with age, some diminish with age, and others remain fairly stable.

Despite differences in the design of the studies cited, their findings point to the following conclusions:

1. Deficits in abstracting (conceptual) and perceptual abilities were found more frequently in school-age children who had suffered perinatal stress.

2. Impairment in gross motor and neurological status was found more frequently among preschool children who had suffered perinatal stress.

TABLE 2   Effects of Perinatal Complications at School Age

Investigator	Child's Age at Follow-up	Neurological	Motor	Perceptual	Intelligence	Personality	Reading
		Type of Impairment[a]					
Darke (1944)	2.5–11.8 years	—	—	—	+	—	—
Stevenson (1948)	5–8 years	0	?	—	—	+	?
Corah et al. (1965)	7 years	0	+	+	0	+	0
Fraser et al. (1959)	7–11.5 years	+	+	+	0	0	0
Bolin (1959)		—	—	—	—	+	—
Schachter, F. et al. (1959)	8 years	?	—	+	+	0	—
Benaron et al. (1960)	3–19 years; Median 10.2	?	—	0	+	+	—
Benaron et al. (1953)	5–15 years; Median 11.7	—	—	—	+	—	—
Schachter, M. (1950)	3–18 years; prepuberty	—	—	—	+	+	—
Arenberg (1960)	5–12 years	—	0	0	0	0	—
Campbell et al. (1950)	8–11 years	—	—	—	0	—	—
Usdin et al. (1952)	13–14 years	—	—	—	0	—	—
McPhail et al. (1941)	School-age	—	—	—	0	0	—
Keith et al. (1960)	10–14 years	—	—	—	0	—	—

NOTE: Reprinted, by permission of the American Academy of Pediatrics, from E. E. Werner, J. M. Bierman, F. E. French, K. Simonian, A. Connor, R. S. Smith, and M. Campbell. 1968. Reproductive and environmental casualties: A report on the 10 year follow-up of the children of the Kauai pregnancy study. *Pediatrics* **42**: 112–127.

[a]Presence of significant impairment reported by investigator is indicated by (+), absence by (0), suggestive by (?), and a dash indicates impairment not studied.

3. Problems of behavior were found in both early and later childhood among children who had suffered perinatal stress, but little information was reported on the quality of the environment in which the children grew up.

4. Results were most inconsistent in studies of the effects of perinatal complications on intelligence. About half of the prospective studies reported lower mental test scores for both preschool- and school-age children who had undergone perinatal stress than for normal controls; the differences for school-age children, however, were less pronounced.

Realizing the possible effects of the environment, some of the investigators (notably Graham et al. 1962; Corah et al. 1965) controlled for the influence of socioeconomic status. However, the cumulative effects of perinatal complications and quality of the family environment on cognitive development have not been adequately analyzed.

THE KAUAI STUDY

The Kauai study complements and extends previous longitudinal research on the relationship between perinatal complications and child development in three major respects: *all* of the children in a whole community were observed rather than small selected samples; the observations began as early as the fourth week of gestation; and *both* perinatal stress *and* the quality of the environment were assessed, and their relative effects on the children's short- and long-term development were evaluated.

CHAPTER 2

The Island of Kauai

THE HISTORY

Kauai, known as the "Garden Island," lies at the northwest end of the main islands in the Hawaiian chain, some 100 miles and a 27-minute jet flight from Honolulu. Roughly circular in shape and about 30 miles in diameter, it is the westernmost county of the United States (figure 1).

Kauai has great natural beauty and is regarded by many people as the loveliest of the islands of Hawaii. It is the oldest of the inhabited Hawaiian Islands, historically as well as geologically, and was the last of the independent Hawaiian kingdoms.

The first landing in Hawaii of the English navigator, Captain James Cook, occurred on Kauai in 1778, and in the years that

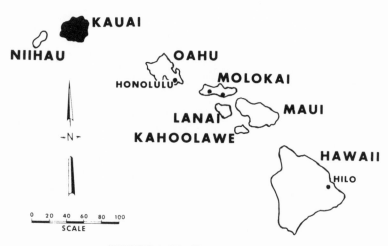

FIGURE 1. The Hawaiian Islands

followed an increasing number of vessels stopped at the island's port of Waimea to trade and replenish their supplies. The first Christian mission was established on Kauai in 1820, and New Englanders set about teaching royalty and, later, the common people to read and write in their native tongue and in English.

In 1835, three Americans established on Kauai the first permanent sugar plantation in the islands, on about 1,000 acres leased to them by a king of Kauai (Kauikeaouli). Koloa Plantation is still in operation today. Sugar soon became the leading source of Hawaii's income. The native Hawaiian population, in the meantime, was diminishing rapidly because of diseases introduced by the white man and had been reduced by approximately 75 percent by the time an official census was taken in 1853 (Lind 1967).

Imported sources of labor had to be sought by the plantation owners. A few Chinese had already settled on Kauai by the 1850s, some engaged in trade and some in growing rice. Portuguese laborers—recruited largely from Madeira and the Azores and imported with their wives and children—began to arrive in large numbers between 1878 and 1887. In contrast to the Chinese, the Portuguese were willing to continue working for the plantations after their original contracts had expired. They also did their part in replenishing the dwindling population.

Far cheaper, however, was the importation of Japanese, rather than Portuguese, to work on the plantations. At first the diligence, adaptability, and thriftiness of the Japanese earned them a cordial welcome; but when they began to arrive in large numbers during the 1890s they appeared to present as much of a labor and population threat as the Chinese had seemed to pose earlier. By the turn of the century, nearly 40 percent of the population was Japanese. This proportion remains about the same today for the state of Hawaii as a whole, though it is slightly higher on Kauai where about 43 percent of the people are of Japanese descent.

Several thousand Puerto Ricans, Koreans, and Spaniards were brought to Hawaii during the early 1900s, but most of the Spanish immigrants left for California when their contracts ended. Beginning in 1907, large numbers of Filipino men were brought in, the majority without wives or families. The purpose of these importations from the Philippines, which continued until 1931, was to provide an additional source of labor. The new arrivals also served as a buffer against the impact of strikes which had harrassed the plantations. Again, in 1946, a large group of Filipinos was brought in to ease the wartime labor shortage. The current excess of males over females on the island, amounting on Kauai to a ratio of almost two to one in the population over 40 years of age, is largely due to the recruitment of Filipino laborers during the present century. The Filipino population is about twice as large on Kauai (25 percent) as in the state of Hawaii as a whole (12 percent).

Figure 2, taken from A. Lind's *Hawaii's People* (1955) shows the population of the Hawaiian Islands, from the date of their discovery by Captain Cook to the beginning of this study.

The rate at which different immigrant groups have advanced up the socioeconomic ladder has varied. The Caucasians of northern European and American ancestry (*haoles*) differed from the other immigrants, inasmuch as they came to Hawaii not as plantation laborers but to fill upper- and middle-class positions, first as missionaries, then as businessmen and plantation managers and supervisors.

The Caucasians, the Chinese, and the Koreans have been the most mobile socially, followed closely by the Japanese who are predominant in the middle classes of the islands. The Portuguese, Puerto Ricans, and Filipinos have been the least mobile socially; together with the Hawaiians and part-Hawaiians they are found predominantly in the lower and lower-middle classes. Relative to their length of stay on the island, the Filipino and Portuguese have shown a slower rate of upward mobility than the other ethnic groups. The Japanese, in contrast, have moved quickly from plantation labor to supervisory, professional, and business posi-

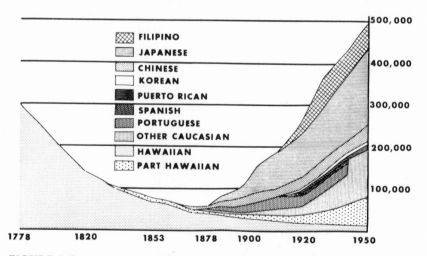

FIGURE 2. Population of the Hawaiian Islands, 1778–1950, by ethnic groups
Reprinted, by permission of the University of Hawaii Press, from A. W. Lind, *Hawaii's People* (Honolulu, 1955), p. 16.

tions, a trend noted also on the United States mainland in California and Chicago (Norbeck and De Vos 1960).

As the new settlers from both East and West began to arrive in increasing numbers, all with their distinctive languages, customs, styles of dress, and food habits, a process of ethnic amalgamation began which has been continuing ever since. New arrivals mastered the island dialect, a modified form of pidgin-English with many Hawaiian words and unusual uses of common English words and phrases. The tendency to remain separate which still persisted among people of different national backgrounds was broken down especially rapidly during World War II. The second and third generations now strongly identify with American ways of living. At the same time the proportion of foreign-born has been declining rapidly.

Of all the births occurring on Kauai during our study, 34 percent were of Japanese ancestry, 24 percent Hawaiian and part-Hawaiian, 18 percent Filipino, 6 percent Portuguese, and 3 percent Anglo-Saxon Caucasians. The remaining 15 percent were principally mixtures of ethnic groups other than Hawaiian, mostly children of Japanese-Filipino parentage, and a few children of Chinese, Korean, and Puerto Rican descent.

THE PEOPLE

The people of Kauai, numbering close to 28,000, live in small towns and plantation camps that are scattered around the shoreline and are connected by a highway which reaches three-quarters of the way around the island, ending in the north where cliffs rise steeply from the ocean's edge. Most of the rainy central part of the island is uninhabited.

Although three-fourths of the population is classified as living in rural areas, a visitor is immediately impressed with much of the island's distinctly suburban atmosphere. People speak of "going downtown" when they plan to board a plane for Honolulu, and these same planes bring thousands of mainland visitors to the island each year.

Agriculture is the principal "industry," the skills it requires are those of a large-scale industrial enterprise. Both the sugar plantations and the pineapple growers run "factories in the field." Sugar represents year-round employment, while pineapple harvesting and canning reach a peak during the summer months when a large number of women are employed in the canneries, often in night shifts.

The second-largest field of employment is in government service (mostly county and state) though retail trade, construction, and the tourist industry have been increasing in recent years. With the exception of the union jobs on the plantations, pay scales are rather low and the economy of the island has been somewhat depressed in recent years.

Except for clothing and housing, for which requirements are minimal because of the consistently mild climate (the average temperature throughout the year is 70° F), the cost of living is high because a large proportion of goods must be shipped from the mainland. Nearly half of Kauai's dwellings in 1950 were plantation houses, but since then there has been a notable increase in the building of private homes. Most households are surrounded with flowers and fruit-bearing shrubs and trees, and many families raise vegetables and keep chickens and sometimes pigs; fishing is a common avocation. *Kokua* ("help or cooperation") is generously practiced, with surplus food or needed services being freely given to friends, neighbors, and relatives. To people who come to Kauai from the mainland, life appears to be easy and leisurely. Many of the pressures of big city existence are absent and simple recreational activities abound.

THE HEALTH AND EDUCATIONAL FACILITIES

Excellent provisions have long been available on the island for health and medical care. When this study began, there were 13 physicians on Kauai, seven associated with the plantations, four in private practice, and two serving as government physicians. The health department had a supervisor of public health nursing with a staff of seven qualified nurses. Two of the eight plantations on the island also employed a nurse whose functions were comparable to those of a public health nurse. Virtually all plantation employees and their families were enrolled in either plantation medical care and hospitalization plans, or in the Hawaii Medical Service Association, an affiliate of the National Blue Shield Association.

Virtually all pregnant women on the island had ready access to prenatal care in a physician's office or dispensary, delivery in the two general hospitals on the island, and medical and hospital care for their infants. In 1955, Kauai's birth rate was 24.8 per 1,000 population, comparing closely with the rate of 24.6 for the United States as a whole. The infant mortality rate was lower than that of the mainland.

At the time of our last follow-up at age 10, Kauai had 15 elementary schools: 11 public and 4 parochial. Four public schools had special classes for educable and trainable mentally retarded children, and there was a Child Training and Rehabilitation Center for severely retarded youngsters. The school district employed a psychological tester for diagnostic work and guidance personnel. A mental health clinic was maintained in the county seat (Lihue), with a permanent staff consisting of a social worker, a clinical psychologist, and a part-time psychiatrist.

The State of Hawaii Department of Health provided on Kauai diagnostic, therapeutic, and remedial services through specialists from Honolulu who conducted clinics in child development, pediatrics, orthopedics, mental retardation, cerebral palsy, and other special fields. For the most part, referrals to these clinics were made by family physicians or by public health nurses as a result of home visits or child health conferences. Where necessary, children were also taken to Honolulu for special diagnostic procedures or treatment.

Our search for a suitable location for our study led us to the island of Kauai. Here we found a high degree of stability of the population, a minimal influence of unfavorable factors on pregnancy outcomes, good coverage of the population by public health and medical care services, interest and active cooperation of the Hawaii State Department of Health and the Kauai district health office, and an unusually helpful and interested community. Also present was a rich opportunity to study a variety of cultural influences on childbearing and childrearing.

The promise of a stable sample proved to be justified. At the time of the two-year follow-up, 96 percent of the living children were still on Kauai and available for study, and for the ten-year follow-up we were able to locate 90 percent. Less than .5 percent of more than a thousand families contacted when the children had reached age 10 refused to participate in the last follow-up.

CHAPTER 3

Methodology

THE CENSUS

In the first phase of the study, five nurses and one social worker, all resident on Kauai, set about obtaining a household census (Yerushalmy et al. 1956). They listed the occupants of each dwelling and recorded demographic information and brief personal data, including a reproductive history of all women 12 years of age and older. Those of childbearing age were asked if they were pregnant; if so, the date of their reported last menstrual period was recorded. A pregnancy-report card with a postage-free envelope was left with each woman, with the request that she mail it to the Kauai District Department of Health as soon as she believed herself to be pregnant.

The local physicians were asked to submit monthly a list of the mothers who had come to them for prenatal care. The physicians were supplied with special forms, serving as a source of pregnancy reports to the study.

CAMPAIGN FOR EARLY PREGNANCY REPORTS

The earliest possible reports of pregnancy were those made by women after their first missed menstrual period. Special efforts were made to encourage early reporting (French et al. 1958). Three local community organizers talked to women's groups and church gatherings in various parts of the island, and a reporter's services were engaged to help with frequent newspaper releases. Community leaders were brought together for a meeting at which the study was explained, and the continued help of the physicians was solicited at a session of the county medical society. Letters were mailed to all women of childbearing age, urging them, when in early pregnancy, to see their physicians and to return an enclosed report card informing us of their pregnancy. Milk cartons

14

delivered to households were bedecked with a printed message urging the mothers to cooperate with the pregnancy study. A series of mother- and baby-care classes were organized by the health department, and nurses went from door to door asking women if they or their friends were interested in such classes—and if they were pregnant. The job of finding new pregnancies continued with radio talks, slides shown in the local movie theatres, posters, and mimeographed throwaways.

Late in 1954 and early in 1955, letters were sent to the women, thanking them for their past cooperation and enclosing once again a report card and envelope. The Kauai District Health Department laboratory, from which prenatal serology was ordered by the physicians, became an additional source of reports. The next letter sent to the mothers, at the end of 1955, contained a calendar decorated with pictures of Kauai babies and a report card. The campaign for early reporting continued until the end of 1956 when the number of pregnancies for study and follow-up was considered adequate.

POPULATION STUDIED

A total of 3,735 pregnancies was reported, of which 2,203 consisted of all women with pregnancies beginning in 1954, 1955, and 1956. These resulted in 240 fetal deaths and 1,963 live-born. These live births will be referred to in this report as the cohort of 1955 (857 births) and the cohort of 1956–1957 (1,106 births).

THE PERIODIC INTERVIEWS

The campaign to get women to report as soon as they believed themselves to be pregnant was conducted once each trimester, simultaneously with the periodic interviews of all women reported pregnant. The interviewers—public health nurses and social workers—were local residents who knew the community and had the trust and cooperation of the mothers. They were trained by the resident research director (a sociologist) in the use of specially prepared interview forms. Additional interviews were held with the mothers during the postpartum period and when the infant was about one year old.

ASSESSMENT OF PERINATAL COMPLICATIONS

A clinical perinatal rating, based on the presence of conditions thought to have had a possible deleterious effect on the fetus or newborn, was made for each child. After reviewing the extensive records, a pediatrician on the research staff scored the severity of some 60 selected complications or events which could occur during the prenatal, labor, delivery, and neonatal periods as follows: 0—not present, 1—mild, 2—moderate, and 3—severe. (A summary of the scoring system for prenatal-perinatal complications is presented in appendix 1.) After all conditions were scored, the pediatrician assigned to each infant an overall score from 0 to 3. This was based on clinical judgment taking into consideration the number, type, and severity of unfavorable conditions present. In general, the numerical value of this overall score is the same as the value assigned to the most severe condition present. Cases with overall scores of 2 and 3 were reviewed by a second pediatrician, and all scoring was checked by a statistician for consistency.

The prenatal interviews, and prenatal, hospital, labor, delivery, and newborn records from the local physicians, as well as livebirth and death certificates, were also included in the records of the study.

THE FOLLOW-UP AT TWO YEARS

In 1956 the first group of babies born to mothers who had been interviewed during their pregnancies was given pediatric and psychological examinations. The study staff and the public health nurses made strenuous efforts to examine every child. The fact that 97 percent (1,666 of the 1,713 liveborn children of the 1955 and 1956–57 cohorts still residing on the island) were examined attests to their success.

Two practicing pediatricians from Honolulu, both diplomates of the American Board of Pediatrics, periodically came to Kauai to conduct the medical examinations. The median age at examination was 19½ months, with 95 percent of the children examined *before* age two. The examinations, based on a systematic appraisal of all organ systems, were conducted principally to assess physical status and to search for congenital and acquired defects. Nutrition, sleeping and feeding habits, toilet training, speech, social and motor development were also appraised. In addition to recording specific findings, the pediatricians were asked to indicate their impressions of each child's overall physical and intellectual status by rating him as superior, normal, low-normal, or retarded, in each area. The pediatricians' judgments were based on their examinations, observations of the children's behavior, and questioning of the mothers. They also recorded their recommendations for further study by the children's physicians or by a specialist provided by the Crippled Children's Branch of the Children's Health Services Division.

For approximately one year, children receiving the special pediatric examinations were routinely given an independent psychological examination. The 734 children examined on this routine basis make up 97 percent of the cohort of 1955 births. An additional 197 children of the cohort of 1956–57 births, or 21 percent of the children who reached the age of examination during the second part of the study, were given psychological examinations (table 3). Having only limited time available from the psychologists, we found that it was not possible to adhere to our original plan of providing routine psychological evaluations for the entire second-year cohort. The 197 children who were examined were mainly selected by the pediatricians because they appeared to fall either below or above the average range of intelligence. The median age for the psychological evaluations was 20 months for those routinely examined and 23 months for the selected group.

Two psychologists from the University of Hawaii, each responsible for half of the group, performed about 90 percent of the psychological evaluations. The remaining children were also tested by well-qualified examiners. The tests given were the Cattell Infant Intelligence Scale (Cattell 1940) and Doll's Vineland Social Maturity Scale (Doll 1953), resulting in Intelligence Quotient (IQ) and Social Quotient (SQ) scores. A specially prepared consultation form covering the sensory and motor status of the child was completed, and a checklist of adjectives was provided to describe both the parent-child relationship and infant behavior patterns observed during the examination. At the end of the examination, the psychologists also recorded a clinical rating of each child's current intellectual status by checking one of the following categories: above normal, normal, questionable, below normal.

THE FOLLOW-UP AT 10 YEARS

All existing sources of information about the children (their physicians, the hospitals, the schools, the health and welfare departments, and, of course, their parents) were utilized in the 10-year follow-up. The local study staff, consisting of a pediatrician, a clinical psychologist, a public health nurse, and part-time interviewers and clerical personnel, was widely known and trusted. All, with the exception of the pediatrician, were residents of the island. Thanks to their efforts and the cooperation of the

TABLE 3 Number of Children in Two-Year Follow-up Study

Type of Examination	Total Live-born in Time Sample	Not Available for Examination[a]	Available for Examination	Not Examined	Received Examination
Pediatric					
TOTAL, Cohorts of 1955 and 1956–1957	1963	250	1713	47	1666
Psychological					
1955 Cohort (on routine basis)	857	99	758	24	734
1956–1957 Cohort (on selection basis)	1106	156	950	753	197
TOTAL	1963	255	1708	777	931

[a]185 moved, 35 died, and 30 mothers were not interviewed during pregnancy. This interview was a prerequisite to follow-up in the study. Although records for these are not as complete as for others, some information pertinent to the present study is available for all.

community, nearly 90 percent of the island's live births occurring in 1955 could be reached 10 years later in 1965–66. One thousand and twelve children participated in the 10-year follow-up, 262 of whom were "high risk" children from the cohort of 1956–57 births. The "high risk" group includes all the two-year survivors in this cohort who had substantial birth defects, injuries, or handicaps, birth weight under 2,500 grams, two-year IQ scores under 85, and those considered by the examining pediatrician or psychologist to be mentally "below normal" at age two.

The mean age of the 1,012 children at the time of the follow-up was 10 years six months, with a range from nine to 11 years. Table 4 shows the study groups for the 10-year follow-up.

The design we followed in the final study utilized the experience we had gained in a pretest in which all procedures were tested with 75 children slightly older than the study group. As a result of this experience, we eliminated the routine pediatric examination we had originally planned for each child because we discovered no findings pertinent to the study beyond those recorded in the extensive medical and school health records already available. The field staff collected information about each of the 1,012 children from the following existing sources:

1. Records of the Crippled Children's Branch, the Mental Health Services Division, the Department of Social Services, and the schools' department of special services.

2. School records including grades, results of previous intelligence and achievement tests, and of speech, hearing, and vision examinations conducted at the school.

3. Records of physicians and hospitals for children who had physical handicaps, illnesses, or accidents.

The staff obtained new information about each child from:

1. A questionnaire filled out by his current teacher, including grades in reading, arithmetic, and writing (grammar and spelling), and a checklist of physical, intellectual, and emotional problems observed in the classroom. (A copy of the teachers' questionnaire appears in appendix 2.)

2. A home interview with the mother covering illnesses, accidents, and hospitalizations in the interval between 2 years and 10 years of age; changes in the home environment; the mother's impressions of the child's school performance; and behavior problems observed at home (see appendix 3).

3. Results of two group tests, the Science Research Associates

TABLE 4   Number of Children in 10-Year Follow-up Study

TIME SAMPLE: LIVE BIRTHS OF 1955

Total Number of Live Births in Cohort	837	
During first two years: died, 12; confidential adoptions, 4; moved from Hawaii, 20		
Total Number Living in Hawaii at Age Two	801	95.7%[a]
From two to ten years of age: died, 3; moved from Hawaii, 45; parents refused follow-up, 3		
Total Number of Children in Follow-up Study at Age 10	750	89.6%[a]

SELECTED SAMPLE: LIVE BIRTHS OF 1956–1957

Total Number Living in Hawaii at Age Two	276	
From two to ten years of age: died, 2; moved from Hawaii, 10; parents refused follow-up, 2		
Total Number of Children in Follow-up Study at Age 10	262	94.9%[b]

COMBINED SAMPLES

Total Number of Children in Follow-up Study at Age 10	1012

NOTE: Adapted, by permission of the American Public Health Association, from F. E. French, A. Connor, J. M. Bierman, K. Simonian, and R. S. Smith. 1968. Congenital and acquired handicaps of 10 year olds: Report of a follow-up study, Kauai, Hawaii, *American Journal of Public Health* 58: 1388–1395.
[a]Percentage of total live births in cohort.
[b]Percentage of selected children living in Hawaii at age two.

(SRA) Primary Mental Abilities Test, Elementary Form (Thurstone and Thurstone 1954) and the Bender-Gestalt test (Smith and Keogh 1962), administered and scored by qualified examiners according to standard directions (Koppitz 1964).

The staff first examined older children in order to equalize age at time of screening examinations. When the Primary Mental Abilities (PMA) test was given, two-thirds of the children were 10 years of age and over 80 percent were in the fifth grade.

A panel of the resident staff, consisting of a pediatrician, a psychologist, and a public health nurse, reviewed each child's record to determine if the information was complete and if there was evidence of any physical defect or handicap, or evidence of any intellectual or emotional problem. They determined whether further diagnostic procedures were needed to complete their appraisal of the child's status at age 10. The panel judged that 299 children (30 percent) needed additional diagnostic examinations. Each examination was then conducted by an appropriate specialist (psychologist, pediatrician, neurologist, audiologist, opthalmologist). Psychological examinations made up the largest number (about two-thirds). A variety of individual tests were used: the Wechsler Intelligence Scale for Children (WISC), individual Bender-Gestalt, Draw-A-Person, Graham-Kendell Memory for Design, Rorschach, Thematic Apperception Test (TAT). In addition to psychological tests, pediatric examinations (20 percent), tests of speech, hearing, and vision (7 percent), and examinations which utilized the services of other specialists (11 percent) were conducted.

The combined screening and diagnostic information was again reviewed by the panel. They prepared a final assessment of each child's status, estimating the effect of any existing handicap on school progress and the need for various types of future care. Data were obtained on all parameters for all children, including those in institutions.

The following types of problems were identified:

School achievement problems. Current grades of D or F in reading, writing, or arithmetic; grade placement one year or more below chronological age; in special class or institution for the mentally retarded or the educationally handicapped.

Intellectual problems. IQ below 85 on the SRA Primary Mental Abilities Test or the WISC.

Perceptual problems. Group Bender-Gestalt error score of four or more (according to the Koppitz Developmental Scoring System 1964), and PMA factor *P* (perceptual acuity and speed) or *S* (space) more than one standard deviation below the total PMA IQ.

Language problems. A marked discrepancy (more than one standard deviation) between verbal and nonverbal subtests on the PMA or WISC, with the verbal subtests inferior to the nonverbal.

Emotional problems. Following are the types of emotional problems identified through the behavior checklists filled out by parents and teachers and confirmed by personality tests administered by clinical psychologists: (*a*) chronic nervous habits—tics; compulsive, persistent mannerisms; thumbsucking, nailbiting; stammering or stuttering; lisping or other infantile articulation defects; (*b*) hyperkinetic symptoms—extremely hyperactive, unable to sit still; marked inability to concentrate, distractible; extremely irritable; (*c*) persistently withdrawn—shy, lack of self-confidence; feelings hurt easily; very unhappy, depressed most of the time; unusual fears or anxieties; (*d*) persistently aggressive—acts out problems; constantly quarreling and bullying; overly contrary and stubborn; violent temper; destructive.

Physical problems. The presence of physical health problems was determined by utilizing existing health records and information concerning illnesses and accidents reported by the mother and confirmed by the physician and hospital involved. If additional diagnostic examinations were judged necessary by the panel, referrals were made to appropriate specialists to verify diagnoses. Of the children in the cohort for whom any health problems were noted, almost three-fourths had problems so minor that they interfered little, if at all, with normal functioning. Most of these were allergies which are known to be prevalent in Hawaii. Physical problems considered to be significant were severe congenital defects: spina bifida; atresias of the intestinal, genitourinary, and auditory systems; congenital heart anomalies; cleft lip and palate; cerebral palsy; and developmental defects of the central nervous system. Also included in this category were defects involving vision or hearing, hernia, hydrocele, persistant thyroglossal duct, pilonidal sinus, and orthopedic problems.

It was agreed that the general findings of the study, including those of significance for individual children needing help, would be made available to everyone concerned. Reports of special diagnostic examinations went to the child's physician, psychological examinations to the department of special services of the schools, and letters with suggestions for follow-up where indicated to the parents. With parental consent, reports were also sent to the Mental Health Services Division and other state agencies to initiate therapy or remedial measures. The psychologist gave several reports at meetings of Kauai principals and teachers on the educational and mental health needs of "problem" children identified in the study.

Since the completion of the study, several community action programs and compensatory educational programs have been initiated on Kauai on the basis of the study findings.

CHAPTER 4

Assessment of the Family Environment

ASSESSMENT AT AGE TWO

The children's early environment was rated by using information gained from interviews with the mother. These interviews were conducted by public health nurses and social workers during the prenatal and postpartum periods and one year after the birth of the child; they were conducted by a psychologist during the two-year examinations.

Three factors were singled out to estimate the quality of a child's early environment: socioeconomic status (SES), family stability, and intelligence of the mother. These factors were selected to reflect material opportunities, emotional support, and intellectual stimulation available to the young child—variables that have shown a significant association with children's cognitive development in other longitudinal studies (Sontag, Baker, and Nelson 1958; Bayley and Schaefer 1964; Bloom 1964; Honzik 1967).

Ratings were made independently by two graduate students, one in psychology and one in social work. They read the interviews, abstracted relevant information, and assigned a score on a five-point scale from very high or favorable (1), to very low or unfavorable (5) for each factor.

The following information was used in rating socioeconomic status: father's occupation, standard of living as rated by interviewers during home visit, arrangements for medical care, and degree of crowding in living quarters. Father's occupation was weighted more heavily than the other factors.

Family stability was evaluated using information which gave evidence of family cohesiveness or upheaval and of the type and duration of any instability. Information on the legitimacy or illegitimacy of the child, presence or absence of the father,

24

presence or absence of severely disrupting events in the household, such as marital discord, alcoholism, and emotional disturbance in the parent(s), and long-term separation of the child from the mother without any adequate substitute care-takers was utilized.

An estimate of the mother's intelligence was made from two sources: number of years of schooling she had completed, and the clinical judgment of the psychologist who interviewed her at the time of the two-year follow-up examination. Using years of schooling as the primary factor in rating, we placed a woman in the "high" categories if her education extended beyond high school, and in the "low" categories if she had attended school eight years or less.

The ratings were made independently of any knowledge of the perinatal scores or of the results of the two-year follow-up. The two raters scored 15 percent of the total sample twice, independently of each other, until they had reached a percentage agreement in the high eighties and nineties.

The interrelations between the three environmental ratings were low: correlation coefficient (r): SES/family stability .21; SES/mother's intelligence .33; mother's intelligence/family stability .03.

ASSESSMENT AT AGE 10

Environmental ratings at age 10 were based on standardized interviews conducted by two public health nurses and a social worker who were familiar with the community and trained in the use of the interview. The main purpose of the interviews was to obtain information from the family, preferably the mother, about the quality of the environment in which the child had grown up from the preschool years to age 10.

A clinical psychologist rated this information for all children on three dimensions: socioeconomic status, educational stimulation, and emotional support. Ratings were made on a five-point scale from very favorable (1) to very unfavorable (5).

To rate socioeconomic status, we combined information on the father's occupation, income level (in terms of plantation pay scales), steadiness of employment, and condition of housing. The rating was based primarily on the father's occupation, categorized by one of five groups: (1) professional, (2) semiprofessional, proprietorial, and managerial, (3) skilled trade and technical, (4) semiskilled, (5) day labor and unskilled.

Educational stimulation was rated by considering the opportunities provided by the home for enlarging the child's vocabulary, the quality of language models available, the intellectual interests and activities in the home, the values placed by the family on education, the facilities and help provided by the parents, the work habits emphasized in the home, the availability of learning supplies, books, and periodicals, and the opportunity provided to explore various aspects of the larger environment (library use, special lessons, recreational activities). It was based on selected questions from a schedule first used by Dave and Wolf in a study of the relationship between the quality of the home environment and the intelligence and achievement of fifth graders in Chicago (Dave 1963; Wolf 1964) and adapted for Kauai. Reliabilities for the environmental ratings were very high—r .89 to .95 (Wolf 1965).

To rate emotional support, we examined the information received from the home interview on interpersonal relations between parents and child, opportunities for satisfactory identification, kind and amount of reinforcements used, and the presence or absence of traumatic experiences. Items concerning methods of discipline, ways of expressing approval, tension, and conflict in the family were included among the interview″questions. The items on which the rating was based had been shown to be related to children's cognitive and personality development in the Berkeley and Fels longitudinal studies (Sontag, Baker, and Nelson 1958; Kagen and Freeman 1963; Bayley and Schaefer 1964; Honzik 1967), and the studies by Milner (1951) and Bing (1963) on the relationship between parent-child interaction and the child's verbal ability and reading achievement.

The reliability of the scoring was checked in a pretest of 75 10-year-olds not a part of the Kauai study group. Only those items were included in the environmental ratings in which a percentage agreement in the nineties had been reached by two independent scorers.

All environmental ratings were made independently of any knowledge of the perinatal scores of the children and the results of the ten-year follow-up study. The intercorrelations between the environmental ratings were moderate and ranged from .57 (socioeconomic status/educational stimulation) to .37 (socioeconomic status/family stability).

The environmental ratings made of the study group at age 10 were somewhat lower than those made at age two. Whereas 30 percent of the two-year-olds were rated as living in homes of low socioeconomic status, 55 percent of the 10-year group were rated as such; those in the middle group had decreased from 59 percent to 34 percent; the proportion with the highest ratings remained the same, about 11 percent.

The shift in ratings of socioeconomic status can be explained by the fact that more information was available on the families when the children were 10 than when they were two, and more children had been born, especially in the lower SES homes. Most of the shift results from including income in terms of plantation pay scales in the SES ratings. Thus, most of the semiskilled occupations were placed in the "low" SES brackets. This is a realistic classification, as evidenced by United States census data which show that the median income on Kauai was lower than the rest of the state and lower than the mainland United States (United States 1960). In addition, the economy of the island was somewhat depressed by the closing of several pineapple canneries and plantations after our follow-up at two years.

Although the ratings of "emotional support" when the children were age 10 and of "family stability" when they were age two are not strictly comparable, we noted a slight downward shift from preschool to school-age. Three out of four Kauai families were given a favorable rating in "family stability" when the children were two; only two out of three families received "average" or "above average" ratings in "emotional support" when the children were 10.

This observation on the changes in family stability is similar to that made in the longitudinal study of a thousand families living in Newcastle upon Tyne (Miller et al. 1960). The British investigators reported:

As we watched the changing fortunes of our families, we came to modify our original optimism concerning family stability and cohesion. In the first years we were able to describe four out of every five families as happy and stable. Many, however, were recently established and relatively inexperienced or lived under conditions of strain. And unfortunately, in the next years, we saw many families come under severe stress, some to the breaking point, because one or the other parent was unable to make the adjustment required for a stable family life or suffered misfortunes or a long illness. Also, as we came to know them better, we were increasingly aware, how slowly we reach any understanding of other families and how essential it is to be patient as well as observing.

On Kauai, the downward shift, though present, was not as pronounced as in Newcastle, where 45 percent of the families were having problems by the time the study children had reached age five; moreover, we followed our children to age 10. We judged that most of our families cared adequately for the emotional well-being of their children, but a third of the families showed signs of instability and disorganization.

The rating of "educational stimulation" at age 10 showed that the study families were about evenly divided between those with "adequate" to "high" ratings and those with "low" to "very low" ratings.

The proportion of families at the lower end of the scale is not surprising, considering the rather low educational level of the Kauai population, its rural character, and the large percentage of workers in the semiskilled and unskilled classes. In 1950, median years of schooling completed by Kauai women, ages 25 and over, was eight grades, and for Kauai males, 25 years and over, only six grades. The lower educational level of the men reflects the presence of the older, immigrant sector of the population, especially the Filipinos.

MEASURES OF PARENTAL ABILITY

Because the Department of Education had begun routinely to test intelligence after World War II, we were able to examine the cumulative records of the parents in our study who had attended public or parochial schools on Kauai. Group intelligence-test scores (in the vast majority of cases, the California Test of Mental Maturity) were obtained for 485 parents, representing nearly half of the families who participated in the ten-year follow-up. They had taken these tests when they were between 10 to 15 years old, at an age close to that of their children at the last follow-up. The results of the comparison between intelligence test scores of parents and children are reported in chapter 11.

CHAPTER 5

The Fetal and Perinatal Periods

THE FARTHER WE push back toward the beginning of antenatal life, the more difficult it becomes to obtain information. During the month after the first missed menses, the four–seven-week period of gestation, pregnancies can be clinically recognized. Because, for this study, we received reports of pregnancies from the women themselves, as soon as they suspected they were pregnant, we were able to learn about more pregnancies and more early fetal losses than would have been possible through routine reports from physicians, hospitals, and registrars of vital statistics.

A special effort was made to determine accurately the first day of the last menstrual period (LMP) for each reported pregnancy. Careful checking was done of any discrepancies between the LMP dates obtained from the women and observations recorded by the attending physician(s).

Success of the study staff in obtaining early reports of pregnancies is indicated by the fact that 80 percent of the pregnancies were under follow-up before the 20th week of gestation, 69 percent before the 16th week, and 50 percent as early as the 12th, including 19 percent first reported between four- and eight weeks gestation.

Analysis of a cohort of 3,083 pregnancies occurring between 1953 and 1956 indicated fetal death rates beginning with the four–seven-week period after the LMP. For a smaller cohort of 1,963 babies born alive (the 1955 and 1956 cohorts), mortality rates and the incidence of handicaps of prenatal and natal origin were determined.

FETAL DEATHS

Because of the follow-up nature of the study, fetal losses could be related during each interval of gestation to well-defined groups of

29

TABLE 5 Antenatal Life Table Functions, Pregnancies of 1953–1956

Gestational Age–Interval from Last Menstrual Period (Weeks)	Number of Pregnancies					Estimated Probability per 1000						Fetal Deaths from Gestational Age x to End of Pregnancy
	At Beginning of Interval	First Reported in Interval	Ending in Interval Fetal Death	Ending in Interval Live Birth	Moved in Interval	During Interval Fetal Death	During Interval Live Birth	During Interval Still Pregnant	From 4 Weeks through Specified Interval Fetal Death	From 4 Weeks through Specified Interval Live Birth	From 4 Weeks through Specified Interval Still Pregnant	
4	0	592	32	0	0	108.11	0.00	891.89	108.11	0.00	891.89	237.25
8	560	941	72	0	1	69.90	0.00	930.10	170.45	0.00	829.55	144.79
12	1428	585	77	0	2	44.78	0.00	955.22	207.60	0.00	792.40	80.52
16	1934	337	28	0	2	13.32	0.00	986.68	218.15	0.00	781.85	37.42
20	2241	248	20	1	9	8.47	0.42	991.11	224.77	0.33	774.90	24.43
24	2459	175	8	4	6	3.15	1.57	995.28	227.21	1.55	771.24	16.11
28	2616	98	8	25	4	3.00	9.39	987.61	229.52	8.79	761.69	13.02
32	2677	67	8	72	6	2.95	26.59	970.46	231.77	29.04	739.19	10.15
36	2658	40	9	1074	3	3.36	401.27	595.37	234.25	325.66	440.09	7.42
40	1612	0	11	1601	0	6.82	993.18	0.00	237.25	762.75	0.00	6.82
TOTAL		3083	273	2777	33							

NOTE: Adapted from F. E. French and J. M. Bierman. 1962. Probabilities of fetal mortality. *Public Health Reports* 77: 835–847.

30

women known to have been pregnant. Probabilities of fetal mortality were determined by the life-table method of analysis, the first to our knowledge ever determined for an entire community for the prenatal period (French and Bierman 1962).

Of the pregnancies reaching four weeks gestation, an estimated 237 per 1,000 ended in death of the conceptus, with the monthly rates of loss forming a decreasing curve from a high of 108 per 1,000 women under observation in the four–seven-weeks period, 70 for 8–11 weeks, and 45 for 12–15 weeks, to a low of three losses between 32 to 35 weeks of gestation (see table 5). Stated positively, the chances of a pregnancy ending in a live birth increased from 76 percent at four weeks to 86 percent at eight weeks, 92 percent at 12 weeks, 96 percent at 16 weeks, and 98 percent at 20 weeks gestation.

Unless women are under observation during successive months of pregnancy, as they were in this study, many early fetal deaths are never registered and are therefore not included in official statistics. The startling differences between our estimates of the true risk of fetal loss in the early months of pregnancy compared with familiar fetal death ratios (registered fetal deaths/live births plus fetal deaths) are shown in figure 3.

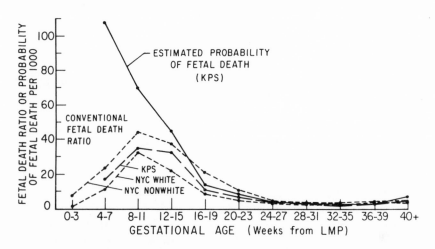

FIGURE 3. Estimated probabilities of fetal deaths per 1,000 pregnancies by gestational age—Kauai pregnancy study, 1953–1956, and study on white and nonwhite populations of New York City, 1958

Reprinted, by permission of C. V. Mosby Co., from J. M. Bierman, E. Siegel, F. E. French, and K. Simonian. 1965. Analysis of the outcome of all pregnancies in a community. *American Journal of Obstetrics and Gynecology* 91:37–45.

Certificates of fetal deaths were registered for 55 percent of the fetal deaths in the study. The percentage increased from 43 percent for those ending four–seven weeks from the last menstrual period to 86 percent for pregnancies ending after 23 weeks.

Another 23 percent were entered in physicians' or hospital records but not registered. In some instances, the expelled conceptus was brought to the physician and pregnancy was confirmed; in others, the woman's description of her early loss was the basis for the physician's diagnosis.

The remaining 22 percent were not recorded in the physicians' records. These losses, like the others, occurred among women whose pregnancies were reported to the study prior to termination of the pregnancy. In some instances the pregnant women had consulted her physician who could not or did not record a diagnosis of pregnancy, and when she made her next visit she was no longer pregnant. Others did not seek medical attention, but reported their losses, as they had reported their pregnancies, directly to the study staff. These women were classified as having fetal losses on the basis of the signs and symptoms they reported.

It should be kept in mind that, because most of the losses occurred so early, the evidence given by the women to the study staff was the same as that given to the physician and used as the basis of his diagnosis. Generally, the women described a period of amenorrhea unusual in terms of their own menstrual histories, followed by abnormal vaginal bleeding of a type consistent with the suspected length of gestation.

Because the only rates we could calculate for the four–seven-weeks period must be based on those pregnancies reported in that interval, we examined those pregnancies as well as those reported at 8–11 weeks to see whether they had characteristics which might be associated with higher-than-usual fetal death rates during the first weeks studied.

We found that most of the characteristics of the women reporting in the early series ordinarily are associated with a lower, rather than a higher, risk of fetal death: they were of a higher socioeconomic status, as indicated by the occupation of the husband; the family size was smaller; the interval from the last pregnancy was somewhat longer; and a larger percentage of the women were married.

To better understand the meaning of our estimates of early fetal loss, we examined reports of laboratory investigations of human ova and of work done on prenatal loss in mammals other than man (Brambell 1948; Perry 1954; Frazer 1955; Hertig et al. 1959).

Although there is no completely satisfactory estimate of total prenatal death rates from fertilization to parturition in any species of mammal, each of these investigators presented evidence supporting a peak rate of loss around the time of implantation. From an intensive study of a small group of fertilized human ova, Hertig and associates estimated a loss of some 40 percent before and during implantation.

The earliest losses we were able to observe (four–seven weeks) probably represented a point on the downward slope of a curve which had been highest 10–14 days earlier. Although we had no comparable longitudinal data with which to compare our estimate of 24 percent eventual loss of the conceptus after four weeks from LMP, it is of interest to note that about 30 percent of the implanted ova studied by Hertig and associates eventually were aborted. Our estimate also was in line with projections made by Ernhardt (1952) based on fetal deaths in New York City. Since our original publication, another prospective life table for the prenatal period has been published (Taylor 1964). It summarizes the experiences of 8,041 women (35 percent Negro, 65 percent Caucasians). Although these were women who had voluntarily reported for prenatal care, monthly probabilities of fetal loss showed the same downward trend from a high during the four–seven-weeks period of gestation.

The rates obtained in our study appear to be reasonable. We believe that they more nearly reflect the true magnitude of early fetal mortality than do measures previously reported.

NEONATAL AND INFANT DEATHS

Neonatal, infant, and second-year mortality rates were all very low on Kauai, reflecting the dramatic reductions in postnatal death rate which have taken place in the state of Hawaii during the last 40–50 years.

The incidence of neonatal and infant deaths in our study group must have reflected a near-minimal effect of unfavorable postnatal influences. There were 13.8 deaths under 28 days per 1,000 single and twin live births. The comparable United States rate in 1960 for deaths under 28 days was 17.2 for the Caucasian and 26.9 for the non-Caucasian population. All of the deaths on Kauai in the neonatal period were attributed to prenatal and perinatal causes, as were four of the 10 remaining deaths occurring from 28 days to two years.

The perinatal mortality ratio, based on fetal deaths of 20 weeks or more plus infant deaths under 28 days, was 35.9 per 1,000 pregnancies; based on fetal deaths 28 weeks and over and first-week deaths, it was 26.1 per 1,000. The preponderance of fetal deaths in the perinatal period is of interest. The number of reported fetal deaths of 20 or more weeks gestation was almost twice the number of neonatal deaths in the first month of life; and fetal deaths limited to 28 or more weeks were some 30 percent higher than deaths of live-born babies which occurred during the first week.

This finding probably reflects the virtually complete reporting of late fetal deaths obtained in the study, and a minimal effect of exogenous factors on early infant deaths. In this respect, the perinatal figures more closely resemble those of Sweden, the Netherlands, and New Zealand (countries with the lowest perinatal mortality rates in the world) than those of the mainland United States (Shapiro and Moriyama 1963).

LOW-BIRTH-WEIGHT INFANTS

The problems of classifying infants whose weight at birth was under 2,500 grams and of isolating the characteristics of the different types have been the subject of considerable recent study (World Health Organization 1961; Gruenwald 1965; Yerushalmy et al. 1965; North 1966).

An editorial in *Lancet* (1966) referred to three kinds of small babies, "those conceived small, those born before their time, and those whose smallness was thrust upon them." We recognized these three categories among the Kauai babies whose birth weights were 2,500 grams or less.

One hundred forty, or 7.4 percent, of the study children weighed 2,500 grams or less at birth. However, 62 of these small babies (3.2 percent of the live births) weighed between 2,301 grams and 2,500 grams and were born after 37 or more weeks of gestation. They were judged by the physicians who delivered them to be, for the most part, the small, normal, full-term babies of small mothers. Only three of this group received special newborn care, remaining in the hospital for a few days after their mothers went home. All survived to age two. These are babies of whom it may be said that they were "conceived small"; that is, their genetic potential for intrauterine growth was less than that for the babies of larger, taller mothers.

Fifty of the small babies, or 2.6 percent of the live births, were born after less than 37 weeks gestation. All but seven of these babies required special newborn care and remained in the hospital for care as prematures for varying periods of time.

Ten of them, all weighing less than 2,000 grams and of less than 32 weeks gestation, died in the first week of life, and there was one additional death in later infancy. These were the true premature infants, those born "before their time."

The third group of 30 babies, 1.6 percent, was born after 37 weeks gestation or more but weighed less than 2,300 grams. Twenty-two of this group required special newborn care and were kept in the hospital. There were four deaths from congenital defects or birth injuries during the first week of life and two additional deaths during later infancy. This group comprised the "dysmature" or "small for date" babies—those who had smallness thrust upon them either by a faulty maternal environment or by abnormal fetal development.

MOTHERS OF LOW-BIRTH-WEIGHT INFANTS

Many investigators have pointed to an increased proportion of birth weights of 2,500 grams or less for certain groups of women. It is not always clear, however, whether such children were born at term or before (Abromowicz and Kass 1966). We studied the incidence of single live births of 2,500 grams or less by length of gestation for 11 variables.

Women with a history of having small babies had the highest proportion of infants weighing 2,500 grams or less for any of the variables studied—4.5 times the incidence for all single births. The incidence was over seven times (33 percent) that for those mothers whose previous babies had been above 2,500 grams (4.5 percent). The same pattern held whether the pregnancy terminated under 37 weeks gestation or later.

We also found a very high proportion of small babies among mothers who had lost weight or gained less than 10 pounds during pregnancy—three times the total incidence. In fact, the more weight our women gained, the lower the proportion of low-weight babies. The incidence decreased from a high of 22 percent for those gaining less than 10 pounds to a low of 2 percent for women gaining 40 pounds or more. Not one of the women who had gained 50 pounds or more had an infant of low birth weight. Women who had been pregnant less than 37 weeks had less time to gain weight, and they accounted for a large proportion of the group with little weight gain; however, even for the women who delivered at term, we found a direct ratio between size of the infant and amount of weight gained by the mother.

Women of short stature delivered small babies almost twice as often as the group in general. The incidence of low-weight infants decreased from 16 percent for women under 59 inches to 3 percent for women at least 67 inches in height. The same pattern held for both preterm and term pregnancies.

A decrease in the proportion of small babies as mothers' prepregnancy weight increased was also demonstrated: 9 percent for mothers weighing less than 100 pounds down to 3 percent for those starting the pregnancy weighing 160 pounds or more. However, this advantage for preterm infants was not evident except for the extremely heavy mothers.

The well-known U-shaped curve showing the incidence of small babies by age of mother and parity was also found. The same pattern held for each gestational group studied except for age of mother: the proportion of small babies born before term was elevated for the very young but not for women near the end of their reproductive period.

The proportion of low-birth-weight babies under and over 37 weeks gestation was approximately twice as high for women unmarried at the beginning of pregnancy as was true for married women.

The percent of babies of 2,500 grams or less did not vary with the interval of time between pregnancies.

To summarize, we found an increased proportion of infants with birth weights of 2,500 grams or less, for gestational ages both under and over 37 weeks, for mothers with a history of small infants, for women who gained little weight during pregnancy, for those of short stature, and for those who were not married at the time the pregnancy began. A history of fetal deaths increased the chance of small, preterm infants only, while low prepregnancy weights were associated more with small, term babies.

Among all of the variables studied, women whose husbands were agricultural laborers (low SES) generally had the highest percentage of small babies. The proportions tended also to be high, in all occupational groups, for women with a history of small infants, and for those not married.

In our population, the relationship of birth weight with ethnic group and the relationship of birth weight with socioeconomic status were not simple. Several factors doubtless played a role in the variations found in the proportion of small babies—from 21 percent for the Puerto Ricans and 11 percent for the Filipinos, to 6 percent for the Japanese and the Hawaiians, and 4 percent for the Portuguese and Anglo-Caucasians. The first two groups—the Puerto Ricans and the Filipinos—who are concentrated toward the lower end of the socioeconomic scale, had the highest proportion of live-born weighing 2,500 grams or less. The Japanese and Anglo-Caucasians were found most often toward the upper end of the socioeconomic ladder, and they had a much smaller percentage of low-birth-weight infants. However, the pattern was reversed for the Hawaiians and Portuguese. Although they tended to have a relatively small proportion of their population in the upper socioeconomic group, they had remarkably low proportions of small babies. Among all these ethnic groups, however, Hawaiian and Portuguese mothers ranked either first, second, or third in average height, prepregnancy weight, weight gain, and gestational age (table 6).

Our observations are consistent with those of Thompson and Billweicz (1963) that tall women have greater reproductive efficiency than do short women. They bear larger, healthier babies than do short women. Thompson and Billweicz also found that heavier women and those who gain more weight during pregnancy have fewer low-birth-weight babies. They regard stature as a useful index of the nutritional and health status of the mother—the result of her lifetime health and nutritional habits plus her genetic potential for growth. Hytten and Leich have found considerable evidence that birth weight depends more on the environment provided by the mother than any other variable (1964). These authors discuss the matter of normal and optimal birth weight, and, citing evidence in terms of infant mortality, show that the larger the baby the more favorable his chances. What is a normal birth weight for an infant must depend on the stature of the mother in terms of risk for the child. The size of the baby must be "normal" for the mother.

POSTMATURITY SYNDROME

More accurate reports of gestational age are needed to study risks associated with the postmaturity syndrome, a subject of continuing controversy.

In our series, where gestational age was carefully determined, postmature infants constituted a larger proportion of the live births than is usually reported (Clifford 1957). Fourteen percent of the babies we studied were of at least 42 weeks gestation; 6 percent of 43 weeks gestation or over; and none were over 46 weeks.

The rates for fetal and first-week deaths were approximately the

TABLE 6 Characteristics of Mothers of Low-Birth-Weight Infants

Ethnic Group of Mother[a]	% of Liveborn			Mother's Mean Height (inches)	Mean Pregnancy Weight (pounds)	Mother's Mean Weight Gain (pounds)	Mean Birth Weight (grams)	Mean Gestational Age (weeks)
	2500 Grams or Less	Gestation under 37 Weeks	Gestation 37 Weeks or More					
Portuguese	3.6(1)	1.2(1)	2.4(2)	62.4(3)	129.2(3)	23.5(3)	3358(2)	40.3(1)
Anglo-Caucasian	4.5(2)	2.3(3)	2.3(1)	64.9(1)	131.1(2)	24.7(2)	3432(1)	40.2(2)
Japanese	5.5(3)	1.9(2)	3.6(4)	60.9(5)	112.7(6)	22.7(6)	3203(4)	39.7(4)
Hawaiian	5.8(4)	2.5(4)	3.3(3)	63.1(2)	137.5(1)	27.3(1)	3299(3)	39.8(3)
Filipino	11.1(5)	3.2(5)	7.9(5)	60.6(6)	113.8(5)	23.0(5)	3036(5)	39.2(6)
Puerto Rican	21.3(6)	8.5(6)	12.8(6)	61.3(4)	127.0(4)	23.4(4)	2990(6)	39.3(5)

[a]Excludes mixed ethnic groups except Hawaiian and part-Hawaiian.

same for gestational ages of 42 weeks or more as for those of 39 through 41 weeks, 14.7 and 13.5 per 1,000 births, respectively. There was no evidence of any greater risk for the postmature infants in terms of all unfavorable outcomes studied, i.e., fetal deaths, deaths under age two, congenital disorders, or central nervous system damage.

It is probable that a relatively small proportion of the true number of births of higher gestational ages are classified correctly in most reported series, many having been erroneously placed in the 40 weeks group. Those designated as 42 weeks or more are likely to have been selected deliberately; attention was called to them because they were considered poor risks.

INCIDENCE OF PERINATAL COMPLICATIONS

Most studies of the relationship between perinatal complications and outcome have compared groups of suspect infants with controls drawn from teaching hospitals (Graham et al. 1957). The incidence of such complications in other than these selected clinical populations is not known.

In Table 7 is shown the overall incidence of live-born babies in our community. For 56 percent of the newborn, the prenatal and perinatal periods were free from complications as we defined them (score of 0). Thirty-one percent suffered complications of only a mild nature (score of 1). For 10 percent, complications of moderate severity were present; and for 3 percent, they were considered severe (score of 3). Among the surviving study children at age two, only 2 percent had severe complications.

Of the infants who died before the two-year follow-up, more than three-fourths (77 percent) were from the very small group with severe perinatal complications. Four-fifths (80 percent) of the deaths among the boys up to age two and two-thirds (67 percent) of the deaths among the girls were due to severe complications. Among the surviving study children, the incidence of perinatal complications by degree of severity was approximately the same for boys as for girls.

Distributions of perinatal score were not significantly different by ethnic group or by age of mother. Out data fail to show a significant association between environmental factors (socioeconomic status, family stability, mother's intelligence) and the incidence of perinatal complications. The fact that Kauai women had easy access to medical care and utilized it freely may be responsible for the lack of social class differences in our study.

TABLE 7 Severity of Perinatal Complications and Survival to Age Two, by Sex

Severity of Perinatal Complications (perinatal score)	Sex	Survived Study Group N	%	Not Examined Na	%	Died N	%	Total N	%
None (0)	M	196	58.5	36	54.6	1	10.0	233	56.7
	F	197	58.8	30	39.0	0	0.0	227	54.7
	M&F	393	58.6	66	46.1	1	7.7	460	55.7
Mild (1)	M	97	29.0	22	33.3	0	0.0	119	29.0
	F	101	30.1	35	45.4	1	33.3	137	33.0
	M&F	198	29.6	57	39.9	1	7.7	256	31.0
Moderate (2)	M	36	10.7	7	10.6	1	10.0	44	10.7
	F	29	8.7	11	14.3	0	0.0	40	9.6
	M&F	65	9.7	18	12.6	1	7.7	84	10.2
Severe (3)	M	6	1.8	1	1.5	8	80.0	15	3.6
	F	8	2.4	1	1.3	2	66.7	11	2.7
	M&F	14	2.1	2	1.4	10	76.9	26	3.1
All Children	M	335	100.0	66	100.0	10	100.0	411	100.0
	F	335	100.0	77	100.0	3	100.0	415	100.0
	M&F	670	100.0	143	100.0	13	100.0	826b	100.0

NOTE: Adapted, by permission of the American Academy of Pediatrics, from E. E. Werner, K. Simonian, J. M. Bierman, and F. E. French. 1967. Cumulative effect of perinatal complications and deprived environment on physical, intellectual, and social development of preschool children. Pediatrics 39: 490–505.

aNinety had no psychological examination primarily because they had moved, and 53 had an incomplete examination (no IQ score obtained).

bExcludes 31 live births with insufficient labor and delivery information for assignment of perinatal score. In no case was there an indication of a complication on the available records.

Other observers studying urban hospital populations have found a higher incidence of perinatal complications among women of low SES (Knobloch and Pasamanick 1959; Perinatal Research Branch 1960–present).

HANDICAPS OF NATAL AND PRENATAL ORIGIN

In order to gain a better idea of the magnitude and nature of nonlethal manifestations of perinatal defects, we classified the children who were born with handicaps of prenatal and natal origin but who survived the first week according to the severity of the handicap and the need for special care. Included were children for whom congenital defects, prematurity, birth injuries, cerebral palsy, convulsive disorders, and severe mental retardation were identified and recorded in the first two years of life. Table 8 shows the 283 children surviving the first week for whom handicaps were recorded in the first two years of life.

In addition to those babies with low birth weights who required no special newborn care (more than half the babies under 2,500 grams in our study), we placed in class I those with minor defects and conditions. These were babies who were not quite perfect, but who could not be considered handicapped and who required little special care (such as babies with skin tabs and hernias). They constituted 7 percent of the live-born in our cohort.

In class II, containing 6 percent of the live-born, are the low-birth-weight babies (predominantly of short gestational age) who required special medical and nursing care during the newborn period. The remaining children in this class required relatively short-term skilled care by specialists, mostly pediatricians, opthalmologists, surgeons, and orthopedists.

Class III comprises the severely handicapped, most of whom had received extensive care by the time of our follow-up at age two. These children suffered handicaps which required long-term, specialized diagnostic and treatment services, special therapy (speech, physical, and occupational) and special education in various combinations. Constituting 3.7 percent of the live-born who survived to age two, they fell into three groups: those with severe physical handicaps, those with both physical defects and severe mental retardation, and children with severe mental retardation identified by age two, but without recognizable physical defects.

Although no significant ethnic differences were found in the overall incidence of congenital defects, significant differences were

TABLE 8 Handicaps of Prenatal or Natal Origin Observed in Children from the Neonatal Period to Age Two

Class	Description of Handicap	Children with Handicap Surviving First Week	
		N	% (of total all classes)
Class I: Minor Handicaps Requiring Little or No Specialized Care	Birth weight 2500 grams or less not requiring special prematurity care	73	25.8
	Minor physical defects and disorders	57	20.1
	Skin tab, 22		
	Umbilical hernia, 12		
	Mild convulsive disorder, 3		
	Other minor defects, 20		
	TOTAL	130	45.9
Class II: Children with Handicaps Amenable to Relatively Short-term Specialized Care	Birth weight 2500 grams or less requiring special prematurity care	57	20.2
	Total with defects	49	17.3
	Strabismus, 24		
	Inguinal hernia, 12		
	Other defects including hydrocele and talipes, 13		
	TOTAL	106	37.5

Class III: Children with Handicaps Requiring Long-term Specialized Care (medical, educational, and custodial)	Total with physical defects	28	9.9
	Spina bifida with meningocele, microcephaly, Sturge-Weber syndrome, and severe strabismus, 5		
	Congenital heart defect, 9		
	Cerebral palsy, Erb's palsy, muscular dystrophy, 4		
	Atresias of gastrointestinal and gastrourological systems, 3		
	Congenital deafness, atresia of auditory canal, congenital diabetes, cleft palate and lip, extensive pigmented mole, and talipes, 7		
	Multiple physical and mental handicaps, including developmental defects of the central nervous system, Mongolism, cretinism, and pituitary dwarfism	10	3.5
		9	3.2
	Mental retardation only (IQs under 70)	47	16.6
	TOTAL	283	100.00
TOTAL ALL CLASSES			

NOTE: Adapted, by permission of C. V. Mosby Co., from J. M. Bierman, E. Siegel, F. E. French, and K. Simonian. 1965. Analysis of the outcome of all pregnancies in a community. *American Journal of Obstetrics and Gynecology* 91: 37–45.

found with respect to the organ systems affected. The Filipino group had the highest incidence of cardiovascular defects and the Hawaiians and part-Hawaiians had the highest incidence of musculoskeletal defects. The Japanese and the Caucasian groups showed significantly lower incidences of skin defects.

EARLY RECOGNITION OF HANDICAPS

Because of its importance to the early recognition of handicaps, we looked at the "yield" of various sources of information available about the children from birth to the two-year follow-up (Bierman, Siegel, French, and Connor 1963).

The children with congenital defects were divided into two groups, those with defects considered to be generally recognizable in newborn infants and those whose defects either were not recognizable at birth or who required special diagnostic skills and procedures. This classification was suggested by a United States Public Health Service study group on congenital malformation statistics (National Center for Health Statistics 1962).

The performance of the physicians on Kauai in their appraisal of the newborn infants was good. Of the 10 with defects considered to be recognizable in the newborn infant on "routine physical examinations by reasonably competent general practitioners" (ibid.), eight were recognized and recorded on the infants' hospital records. They were spina bifida with meningocele, cleft lip and palate, imperforate anus and vagina, mongolism, extensively pigmental mole, polydactylism, and syndactylism. However, only the first four defects were recorded on the birth certificate.

The records of the babies also indicated that 21 of them had defects which are less frequently recognized before hospital discharge. About half of these were of such a nature as to make early recognition especially desirable from the standpoint of treatment and search for associated defects. They included suspected amyotonia congenita, biliary and jejunal atresias, congenital heart defect, persistent thyroglossal duct, and abnormalities of the external ear and canal. Among this group, only five were recorded on the birth certificate.

Thus, less than one-third of the defects noted at birth were so designated on the birth certificate.

In addition to the 29 children with defects reported at birth, defects had been recognized in 37 other children who were being cared for by the family physician or the Crippled Children's

Branch of the Children's Health Services Division before the special follow-up examinations of the study at around age two. These special examinations then brought to light an additional 75 children with handicaps requiring special diagnostic and treatment services.

In most of the severely retarded children in whom there were also physical defects, the retardation was first recognized by the family physician. On the other hand, the children judged to be below normal mentally who were without physical defects were, with one exception, first recognized through the special efforts of the two-year follow-up examination.

CHAPTER 6

The Two-Year Follow-up

OUTCOMES

With a 24 percent probability of fetal mortality, we estimated that for each 1,000 live births on Kauai, there were 1,311 pregnancies which had advanced to four weeks gestation. By age two these 1,311 pregnancies, in turn, yielded an estimated 844 survivors who were free of any physical defects requiring special care and who had IQs of at least 85.

Physical Status

Fourteen percent of the children (13 percent of the boys and 15 percent of the girls) in the 1955 cohort were classified by the examining pediatricians as being "below normal" in physical status at the time of the two-year follow-up examination. Those so designated were found to have either congenital defects, primarily of the central nervous, musculoskeletal, and cardiovascular systems, or to have been born prematurely or "under par" in physical development. Of the infants weighing 2,500 grams or less at birth, 34 percent were judged to be "below normal" in physical status compared to 13 percent for heavier infants.

Intellectual Status

Ninety-three percent of the cohort of 1955 births were rated as "normal" in intellectual status by the pediatricians. Only 1.2 percent were rated as "superior," 4.8 percent as "low normal," and 0.6 percent as "retarded." In contrast to the distribution of the pediatricians' ratings, the Cattell IQs of the 1955 cohort of live births covered a wide range (from 30 to 157), and, as would be expected, were more differentiating. The results indicate that 9.6 percent of the children obtained Cattell IQs of above 115, and 9.4 percent scored below 85.

46

Figure 4 shows the percentage distribution of Cattell IQs and the pediatricians' assessments of intelligence by sex.

The distribution of the IQs and of the pediatricians' assessments of intelligence differed in that a larger proportion of children were rated as "normal" by the pediatricians and a smaller percentage of

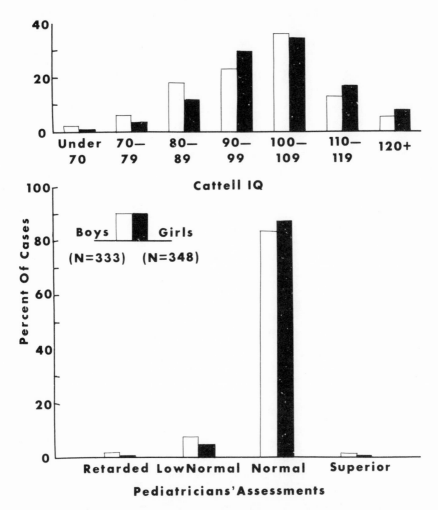

FIGURE 4. Percentage distribution of Cattell IQs and pediatricians' assessments of intelligence: births of 1955, Kauai pregnancy study

Reprinted, by permission of the American Academy of Pediatrics, from J. M. Bierman, A. Connor, M. Vaage, and M. P. Honzik. 1964. Pediatricians' assessments of intelligence of two year olds and their mental test scores. *Pediatrics* 34:680–690.

children were rated by them at the extremes as "superior" or "retarded." The two distributions were in agreement in describing a larger proportion of males than females as "low normal" or "retarded." Twice as many boys as girls had Cattell IQs below 85, and twice as many boys received a clinical rating of "below normal" or "retarded" in intellectual status at age two.

Secular Trends

A comparison of the distribution of the Vineland and Cattell scores is pertinent. Cattell test results were consistent with the norms (girls: mean IQ 100, standard deviation (SD) 12; boys: mean IQ 97, SD 13). The mean SQs for the Kauai children, however, were higher than the Cattell IQs and were almost one standard deviation above the 1935 standardization norms (girls: mean SQ 118, SD 14; boys: mean SQ 114, SD 15). The girls were somewhat more advanced than the boys in their overall level of social competence at this age.

In 1957, preschoolers on Kauai passed about three-fourths of the 27 items in the I–III-year range of the Vineland Social Maturity Scale at an earlier age than the children in the 1935 standardization sample. Most of these items were in the occupation, socialization, and locomotion categories. Our results and those of other investigators using the Vineland Scale in the past two decades point to an acceleration of social competence among preschoolers and young school children, with the girls slightly ahead of the boys (Corah 1965; Werner and Simonian 1966).

These results are consistent with observations by Knobloch and Pasamanick (1960) and Honzik (1962), using other infant and preschool tests which were constructed 30 years ago. Knobloch and Pasamanick found that 40-week-old babies tested with the Gesell Developmental Scales around 1955 scored considerably above the norms in the gross-motor and personal-social areas. Honzik reported that 8–10-month-old infants tested around 1960 scored one standard deviation above the norms of the original Bayley Mental and Motor Scales.

These findings may reflect both a more rapid rate of maturing due to better nutrition and health care and a change in the stimulation provided by the environment since the early 1930s when infants and preschool children were first tested in normative studies.

Some changes may well have come about because of increasing exposure of mothers of all social levels to "expert advice" on the rearing of children, because of widespread access to mass media (magazines, radio, television) and other agents of social change (Bronfenbrenner 1958), and because of a shorter time lag in the assimilation of such cultural influences (Caldwell 1964). That this may hold true for all social levels is illustrated by the lack of socioeconomic differences in measures of social competence. Kauai children of *all* classes had higher mean scores on the Vineland Social Maturity Scale than the 1935 standardization group.

SHORT-TERM EFFECTS OF PERINATAL COMPLICATIONS

Physical Status

As shown in table 9, there is a direct relationship between severity of perinatal stress and the proportion of children rated "below normal" in physical status by the pediatricians. Whereas 11 percent of the children with no perinatal complications were considered to be of "below normal" physical status, 23 percent of the children with moderate perinatal complications and 36 percent of the children with severe perinatal complications were classified in this category. The latter had major congenital defects requiring long-term specialized medical care.

Intellectual Status

As perinatal stress increased in severity, the proportion of children scoring "below normal" on Cattell IQ, Vineland SQ, and clinical ratings also increased. Retardation in cognitive development was especially pronounced for children with moderate to severe perinatal complications.

On the basis of both test performance and observations of the child's behavior, the psychologists rated 29 percent of the children with severe perinatal complications "below normal" and another 29 percent "questionable." Of those with moderate perinatal complications, 22 percent were considered to be "below normal" and 12 percent "questionable."

The differences in mean Cattell IQs between the four perinatal stress groups were statistically significant. Looking at the distribution of the IQs, one is impressed by the increase in the proportion of children with IQs under 85—it more than doubles when one compares the children with no perinatal complications with those who had undergone severe perinatal complications.

In the case of the SQs, no significant differences were found among the perinatal complication groups. However, of the children with perinatal scores of 3 (severe stress), more than a

TABLE 9 Severity of Perinatal Complications for Each of Four Two-Year Criteria

| Two-Year Criteria | Total Children | | Percentage of Children for Each Criterion Classification by Severity of Perinatal Complications | | | | Result of Statistical Test |
	N	%	None (0)	Mild (1)	Moderate (2)	Severe (3)	
Physical Health Status							
Below normal or retarded	95	14.2	10.9	16.2	23.1	35.7	$\chi^2 = 13.37**$
Normal or superior	575	85.8	89.1	83.8	76.9	64.3	
TOTAL	670	100.0	100.0	100.0	100.0	100.0	
Psychologists' Clinical Rating of Intelligence							
Below normal or retarded	90	13.5	11.0	14.6	21.5	28.6	$\chi^2 = 20.36**$
Questionable	56	8.4	6.9	8.6	12.3	28.6	
Normal or superior	521	78.1	82.1	76.8	66.2	42.8	
TOTAL	667	100.0	100.0	100.0	100.0	100.0	

Cattell IQ

More than 1 SD below mean	64	9.6	8.6	8.6	15.4	21.4
Within 1 SD below mean	238	35.5	34.4	35.8	35.4	64.3
Within 1 SD above mean	305	45.5	46.1	48.0	41.5	14.3
More than 1 SD above mean	63	9.4	10.9	7.6	7.7	0.0
TOTAL	670	100.0	100.0	100.0	100.0	100.0
(Mean)	(98.7)	—	(99.4)	(98.6)	(97.6)	(85.5) F=6.24**

Vineland SQ

More than 1 SD below mean	77	11.7	10.3	9.8	20.0	38.5
Within 1 SD below mean	231	35.0	36.9	35.0	26.1	23.1
Within 1 SD above mean	248	37.6	35.8	42.3	38.5	15.4
More than 1 SD above mean	104	15.8	17.0	12.9	15.4	23.1
TOTAL	660	100.0	100.0	100.0	100.0	100.0
(Mean)	(116.7)	—	(117.0)	(116.9)	(115.0)	(111.6) F=1.00

NOTE: Reprinted, by permission of the American Academy of Pediatrics, from E. E. Werner, K. Simonian, J. M. Bierman, and F. E. French. 1967. Cumulative effect of perinatal complications and deprived environment on physical, intellectual, and social development of preschool children. *Pediatrics* 39: 490–505.

**p < .01

third (39 percent) scored more than one standard deviation below the mean of the Kauai sample, compared with only 10 percent of the children with perinatal scores of 0 and 1.

Behavioral Observations

In addition to assessing the children's mental and social status at age two, the psychologists also evaluated "ease or difficulty of rapport" with the child in the testing situation and checked a number of adjectives describing the child's reaction to the test materials, the examiner, and the accompanying person.

Although none of the differences were statistically significant, the following adjectives (from a list of 72) were checked more frequently for children who had undergone severe perinatal stress than for others: "awkward," "bashful," "dull," "hesitant," "impulsive," "inhibited," "slow," and "tense." There were no differences among the various perinatal groups in the rate at which adjectives were checked which commonly are used to describe children with "minimal brain damage" or "hyperkinetic syndrome": "distractible," "excitable," "restless," "persevering," and "temperamental."

However, difficulty in establishing rapport with the examiner (sometimes necessitating a retest) was more frequent among children with moderate and severe perinatal complications. The percentages so described were 12, 14, 18, and 29 for children with no, mild, moderate, and severe perinatal complications respectively.

Findings by Multiple Criteria

In each perinatal group, some children were rated "below normal" in only one area, in two areas, or in all three areas of development.

Sixteen percent of the children were rated "below normal" in intellectual status, 14 percent in physical status, and 12 percent in social competence. Of the children rated "below normal," most were low in only one area of development. However, with increasing perinatal stress, the percentage of children low in more than one area increased (from 6 percent to 29 percent in two areas, and from 1 percent to 7 percent in all three areas of development).

Had the two-year follow-up been restricted to the pediatric examinations, only 46 percent of all "below normal" children would have been detected. Had the follow-up study been limited to the psychological examinations, a little over two-thirds (70 percent) would have been pinpointed. This observation highlights the need for the use of multiple criteria and interdisciplinary cooperation in the assessment of preschool children.

Discussion

Our findings of an increase in the proportion of two-year-olds considered to be "below normal" in physical, intellectual, and social development with increasing severity of perinatal stress agree with reports of other investigators who followed children with perinatal complications into the early preschool years.

The majority of the investigators in other follow-up studies in the English literature have found, as we did, that, among infant and preschool children with histories of perinatal complications, significant impairment was indicated by infant mental and motor tests, individual intelligence tests, tests of concept-formation, perceptual-motor functions, pediatric-neurological examinations, and behavior ratings.

Honzik (1962) found that 23 babies who had been rated definitely suspect on the basis of perinatal complications scored significantly lower than normal controls on the Bayley Mental and Motor Scales at eight months and had special difficulty with items requiring problem solving and eye-hand coordination. They were also significantly more often rated "hypoactive" or "hyperactive," "distractible," and "poorly coordinated."

Stechler (1964), in a series of tests administered to children between 10 weeks and 25 months old, reported the Gesell Developmental Quotient (DQ) of nine apneic children to be lower than that of 17 normal controls in the motor, adaptive, and language areas, but not in the personal-social area.

MacKinney (1958) obtained results similar to ours with the Cattell test given at 6, 12, 18, and 24 months to a group of 24 babies with neonatal asphyxia and to 24 controls.

At three years, Graham et al. (1962) found that anoxic children scored significantly lower than normal controls on all tests of cognitive functioning including the Stanford-Binet, with greatest impairment in conceptual ability. Anoxic children also exhibited significantly more positive and suggestive neurological signs and behavior disturbances. Impairment was more pronounced with postnatal than with prenatal anoxia.

Two European studies used the Griffith Infant Test. Prechtl (1960) in Holland and Ucko (1965) in Great Britain found no significant differences in mean DQs and IQs between children with perinatal complications and normal controls, but reported behavioral differences in the follow-up between two and five years similar to our own observations: a higher incidence of anxiety, negativism, sensitivity, and disequilibrium in the face of change.

Realizing the possible effect of the early environment on outcome, some investigators, notably Graham et al. (1962), controlled for SES. However, the cumulative effect of both perinatal complications and quality of environment was not analyzed.

In the following section we present for our data, drawn from an entire community with a wide range of socioeconomic strata and family environments, an analysis of the relative effect of the quality of early home environment and the degree of perinatal stress on the young child's physical, intellectual, and social development.

EFFECTS OF QUALITY OF HOME ENVIRONMENT

Each of the ratings of the child's early home environment (socioeconomic status, family stability, and the estimate of mother's intelligence) showed a significant association with outcomes at age two, when analyzed in conjunction with degree of perinatal complications.

In general, the more severe the perinatal complications and the more unfavorable the early home environment, the more retarded was the physical and intellectual development of the child by age two. The cumulative effect of both degree of perinatal complications and quality of environment is illustrated in table 10.

Physical Status

Children with severe perinatal stress who came from homes with little family stability or where the mother's intelligence was considered low were more often rated "below normal" in physical status than were children with severe perinatal complications growing up in homes where family stability and mother's intelligence appeared adequate or favorable. There was no consistently unfavorable association between socioeconomic status and "below normal" physical status among the children with perinatal complications, regardless of degree of stress. This may well be a consequence of the easy and free access that Kauai families had to excellent medical and public health facilities. Lack of financial means would not have precluded use of these services, but lack of intelligence and family stability apparently did. A similar finding is reported by Douglas and Bloomfield in a five-year follow-up study of 5,386 British children (1958).

Intellectual Status

Even before they reached their second birthday, children born to mothers rated low in intelligence, or growing up in families low in stability or socioeconomic status, had a substantially higher percentage of "below normal" intelligence ratings than children growing up in a more favorable early home environment. This effect was especially pronounced among children suffering some degree of perinatal stress. Whether perinatal complications were mild, moderate, or severe, children coming from the more deprived homes (intellectually, emotionally, and materially) had a higher proportion of "below normal" intelligence ratings than children reared in a more adequate family environment. The cumulative effect of both perinatal complications and quality of early home environment is seen in table 10 by noting that children with no perinatal stress living in the least favorable environments, and those with the most severe perinatal complications but living in a favorable environment, had comparable mean Cattell IQs.

The effect of a deprived home environment was especially pronounced for children with moderate and severe perinatal stress. The difference in mean Cattell IQs around age two between children with severe perinatal stress growing up in a favorable environment and those with severe perinatal stress growing up in a predominantly unfavorable environment amounted to 16–34 IQ points, depending upon the environmental variable. It was especially dramatic for the socioeconomic status and the family stability ratings.

In contrast, the differences in mean Cattell IQs between children with severe perinatal stress and those without any perinatal complications, growing up in an adequate early environment, though significant, amounted to only six–seven IQ points.

Social Maturity

Low family stability and a low estimate of maternal intelligence showed a significant association with lower mean scores on the Vineland Social Maturity scale, but degree of perinatal stress did not significantly affect the mean SQ at age two.

Discussion

If we look at the evidence that is accumulating in our own and other longitudinal studies on the relationship between the early environment and a young child's cognitive development, it becomes apparent that, besides adverse prenatal and perinatal experiences, variables such as parental language styles, stimulation,

TABLE 10 Percentages of Children Rated "Below Normal" on Two-Year Criteria, by Environmental Factors and Severity of Perinatal Stress

Environmental Variable	Severity of Perinatal Complications				Results of Statistical Test
	None (0)	Mild (1)	Moderate (2)	Severe (3)	LIKELIHOOD RATIO TEST
	PERCENTAGE IN EACH VARIABLE CLASSIFICATION BELOW NORMAL				
For Physical Health Status					
Socioeconomic Status					
Low and very low	12.2	13.8	21.4	66.7	
Medium	10.9	15.9	22.0	22.2	$\chi^2=15.87$
High and very high	7.5	16.7	16.7	50.0	
Family Stability					
Low and very low	26.7	0.0	33.3	66.7	
Medium	6.8	16.7	.7.7	33.3	$\chi^2=29.50^*$
High and very high	11.1	16.0	24.4	25.0	
Estimate of Mother's Intelligence					
Low and very low	20.0	19.5	27.3	50.0	
Medium	8.3	14.6	18.5	28.6	$\chi^2=20.82$
High and very high	8.8	13.6	21.7	33.3	
For Psychologist's Clinical Assessment of Intelligence					
Socioeconomic Status					
Low and very low	8.6	20.7	42.9	66.7	
Medium	10.0	12.1	17.1	22.2	$\chi^2=28.09^*$
High and very high	18.0	4.2	0.0	0.0	
Family Stability					
Low and very low	13.3	40.0	100.0	66.7	
Medium	16.7	14.6	23.1	33.3	$\chi^2=37.80^{**}$
High and very high	8.6	11.4	15.6	12.5	
Estimate of Mother's Intelligence					
Low and very low	12.0	26.8	36.4	50.0	
Medium	13.8	15.7	18.5	14.3	$\chi^2=36.44^{**}$
High and very high	4.9	1.7	17.4	33.3	

	MEAN SCORE (AND STANDARD DEVIATION)				ANALYSIS OF VARIANCE	
For Cattell IQ						
Socioeconomic Status						
Low and very low	98(11)	96(12)	93(12)	61(37)	S	F=11.37**
Medium	100(12)	100(11)	98(14)	91(8)	P	F=6.80**
High and very high	102(12)	100(11)	104(20)	95(13)	SXP	F=2.58*
Family Stability						
Low and very low	96(12)	90(10)	83(6)	77(8)	F	F=9.99**
Medium	99(11)	98(10)	96(8)	73(46)	P	F=7.71**
High and very high	100(11)	100(12)	99(16)	94(6)	FXP	F=1.42
Estimate of Mother's Intelligence						
Low and very low	98(12)	94(10)	89(16)	80(9)	I	F=7.00**
Medium	98(11)	99(12)	97(11)	84(29)	P	F=5.74**
High and very high	102(11)	101(10)	102(16)	96(8)	IXP	F=1.13
For Vineland SQ						
Socioeconomic Status						
Low and very low	116(13)	117(16)	113(19)	102(16)	S	F=0.87
Medium	118(13)	116(12)	113(15)	116(24)	P	F=1.56
High and very high	115(12)	118(11)	119(15)	102(29)	SXP	F=0.97
Family Stability						
Low and very low	117(15)	113(12)	92(7)	89(7)	F	F=9.22*
Medium	116(12)	114(11)	116(13)	127(6)	P	F=3.04*
High and very high	117(13)	118(14)	115(16)	116(24)	FXP	F=2.65*
Estimate of Mother's Intelligence						
Low and very low	115(15)	113(12)	104(19)	94(3)	I	F=10.73**
Medium	117(13)	117(13)	114(14)	117(29)	P	F=2.21
High and very high	118(12)	119(14)	118(14)	123(6)	IXP	F=1.79

NOTE: Reprinted, by permission of the American Academy of Pediatrics, from E. E. Werner, K. Simonian, J. M. Bierman, and F. E. French. 1967. Cumulative effect of perinatal complications and deprived environment on physical, intellectual, and social development of preschool children. *Pediatrics* 39: 490–505.

*p $<$ .05
**p $<$ .01

concern for and emotional involvement with the child, and parental attitudes toward achievement have already made a significant impact *before* a child's second birthday, leading to increasing differences on cognitive measures between children from middle- and lower-class homes.

The findings of MacKinney (1958) and Stechler (1964) seem to suggest that a gradual recovery process is apt to obliterate early differences between survivors of perinatal stress and normal control children, whereas the overwhelming influence of the environment accentuates differences between children growing up in favorable and unfavorable homes.

Much evidence on the effect of environment on intellectual functioning has been reviewed by Hunt (1961), Bloom (1964), McCandless (in Steven and Heber 1965), and Freeberg and Payne (1967). Bloom reevaluated the data from longitudinal studies of the past four decades in an attempt to support a hypothesis of differential growth rate for human intellectual ability. He concluded that, in terms of intelligence measures at age 17, approximately 50 percent of the variance could be accounted for by age four, and that as much intellectual growth was achieved between birth and four years of age as was achieved for the remaining 13 years. The studies that he presented in support of his hypothesis of the effects of environmental deprivation or stimulation on IQ documented changes after ages three and four. Since our data show the effects of both perinatal complications and quality of environment before the children reached their second birthday, we compare here our findings with studies that have dealt with environmental correlates of mental growth in the first two years of life. Taken together, these data seem to suggest that it is necessary to provide enrichment programs much earlier than is currently the practice.

The possibility that a favorable environment has some effect on the child's mental growth as early as the first year is suggested by Yarrow's study (1963) of 40 adopted infants who were tested at six months. Environmental variables that correlated highly with the infants' IQs were stimulus adaptation (the extent to which materials and experiences given to the infant are adapted to his capacities), achievement stimulation, social stimulation, and affectional interchange (the emotional involvement with and acceptance of the infant).

In the California longitudinal studies which began before age two (the Berkeley Growth Study at one month and the Guidance Study at 21 months), both Bayley (1954) and Honzik (1957) found an increasing relationship between all aspects of the socio-economic milieu and children's test performances in the second year of life.

Bayley and Schaefer (1964) also reported significant correlations of early maternal behavior (from birth to three years) with children's IQs around age two. Early ratings of the mother's positive evaluation of and emotional involvement with her child, her expression of affection, her concern about early achievement demands, correlated positively with both boys' and girls' IQs at 18–24 months. Ratings indicating financial strain in the home showed a negative correlation with the child's IQ. Among early ratings of children's behavior, the adjectives "rapid," "responsive," "active," "not shy" correlated positively with the IQs of children of both sexes at 18–24 months. These are the same characteristics that have been noted frequently among Kauai infants who grew up in a postnatal environment rated as favorable (see chapter 8).

Honzik (1967) found increasing correlation between the child's test performance and early evidence of maternal concern, energy, tendency to worry, and concern of both parents with achievement. These family characteristics were evaluated at 21 months and were based on home and office interviews, procedures similar to the ones used in the Kauai study. One of the most clearcut findings from the Berkeley Guidance Study is the accelerative effect of the "energetic," "tense," "concerned," and "worrying" mothers on their children's early cognitive development. Honzik suggests that mothers with these stimulus characteristics probably do more for and with their children and may be more responsive to their needs and wants than are mothers who are lethargic, lack energy, and are not too concerned about their children. Her findings are very similar to our own. Note how often the adjectives "energetic," "concerned," "worrying," "responsible" appear among the descriptions of mothers with children who had higher Cattell IQ scores; conversely, note how often the adjectives "careless," "childlike," "indifferent," "easygoing" are used to characterize mothers whose children had Cattell IQs in the "below average" range (see chapter 8).

In a longitudinal study in Great Britain, Moore (1968) followed London children from six months to eight years and found significant correlations between their IQs and 2½ year ratings of maternal vocabulary, verbal stimulation, and emotional climate in the home, irrespective of social class. Two of the early ratings of the home which proved predictive of children's mental growth up to eight years concerned the kind of stimuli offered to the child:

the toys, books, and experiences available, and the example and direct encouragement to speak.

Many of the social class differences in cognitive development of children which are beginning to be noticeable in the second year of life are likely to center around parental stimulation of the development of language skills. Bernstein (1960) explains these differences along an "elaborative-restrictive" dimension. The "elaborative" language of the middle-class home specifies meaning, makes differences distinct, offers options and alternatives, and builds an increasingly complex conceptual hierarchy for the child. An example of a "restrictive" language is the island dialect of Kauai, a modified form of pidgin English. It is spoken in more than 90 percent of the lower-class families, but only in a minority of middle- and upper-class homes. It has a primitive grammar and word structure, uses simple, concrete verb-noun, verb-pronoun combinations, is repetitive, and makes extensive use of expressive vocal features.

Early and consistent exposure to this type of language can lead to less abstraction and more simple relational responses, as we found in an analysis of language development and reading problems among the Kauai children (Werner, Simonian, and Smith 1967) and as Hess and Shipman (1965) have shown in their study of contrasting verbal styles among middle- and lower-class Negro mothers and their preschool children. "The meaning of deprivation," in the view of these authors, "is a deprivation of meaning" (p. 885).

In sum, although they constitute only a small proportion of all live-born, children suffering from moderate to severe perinatal stress need to be identified early and efforts made to provide them with a supportive and stimulating environment to minimize the effects of the perinatal damage.

But, even more important, we must not overlook the potential benefits of a favorable early environment for the much larger group of children without perinatal stress who are born into unfavorable homes. As the damaging effects of a poor postnatal environment are already apparent by age two, it is necessary to provide enrichment programs much earlier than is currently the practice. Attempts at intervention, whether daycare programs in infancy (Caldwell 1964), transfer to a more stimulating environment (Skodak and Skeels 1949; Skeels 1966), or specific parental instruction in the use of language and reading skills (Irwin 1960), may well be more fruitful in the second year of life when the child turns from sensory-motor manipulation of objects to the acquisition of concepts.

CHAPTER 7

The Ten-Year Follow-up

OUTCOMES

The estimated 1,311 pregnancies for each 1,000 live births on Kauai yielded 660 children who at age 10 were functioning adequately in school and had no identifiable physical, intellectual, or behavioral problems. Thus, during the intrauterine period, birth, and the first decade of life, the reproductive and environmental casualties among the young in this community amounted to about one-half of the children conceived and to about one-third of the live-born.

Learning, Behavioral, and Physical Problems

Table 11 gives an indication of the magnitude of the achievement, intellectual, emotional, and physical problems at age 10 for the 1955 cohort of 750 children. Forty percent of the children received grades of D or F in one or several of the basic skill subjects (reading, grammar, spelling, arithmetic). In each subject, more than one-fourth of all the children had grades of D and about 5 percent had Fs. The most frequent problem encountered among Kauai children at this age was an inability to read satisfactorily. More than one-third (37 percent) of the study group received grades of D or F in reading; about one out of six read at a level of one grade or more below chronological age (CA). Twice as many boys as girls had serious reading problems (Fs: 2.4 percent of the boys, 1.3 percent of the girls; reading below CA: 19 percent of the boys, 9.4 percent of the girls), a trend noted in other studies on the United States mainland (Miller, Margolin, and Yolles 1957; Eisenberg 1966).

Ten percent of the children were in a grade below their chronological age and 2.3 percent were in special classes for the mentally retarded or in institutions. Girls had fewer achievement

TABLE 11   Percentages of Children with Achievement, Learning, Emotional, and Physical Problems at Age 10, by Sex

	Percentage with specified problem			Results of Chi-Square Test
Type of Problem	Boys N=369	Girls N=381	Total N=750	
One or More School Achievement Problems	51.0	37.0	43.9	$\chi^2 = 14.37$**
D or F in reading, writing, or math	46.9	33.6	40.1	$\chi^2 = 13.21$**
One or more grades below CA	13.0	6.0	9.5	$\chi^2 = 10.33$**
In mentally retarded class or institution	2.4	2.1	2.3	$\chi^2 = .10$
One or More Problems Learning	26.0	20.5	23.2	$\chi^2 = 3.12$
IQ below 85	11.4	10.0	10.7	$\chi^2 = .35$
Perceptual problem	11.4	12.6	12.0	$\chi^2 = .22$
Language problem	9.2	4.7	6.9	$\chi^2 = 5.63$*
One or More Emotional Problems	30.9	22.0	26.4	$\chi^2 = 7.12$**
Chronic nervous habits	8.4	5.0	6.7	$\chi^2 = 3.39$
Hyperkinetic symptoms	8.7	3.2	5.9	$\chi^2 = 10.14$**
Persistently withdrawn	9.5	8.1	8.8	$\chi^2 = .41$
Persistently overaggressive	7.3	6.8	7.1	$\chi^2 = .06$
Other emotional problems	4.3	3.2	3.7	$\chi^2 = .00$
Significant Physical Handicap	6.0	6.0	6.0	$\chi^2 = .00$

NOTE: Reprinted, by permission of the American Academy of Pediatrics, from E. E. Werner, J. M. Bierman, F. E. French, K. Simonian, A. Connor, R. S. Smith, and M. Campbell. 1968. Reproductive and environmental casualties: A report on the 10 year follow-up of the children of the Kauai pregnancy study. *Pediatrics* **42**: 112–127.

*p < .05
**p < .01

problems than boys and a smaller proportion placed in grades below their chronological age. About 11 percent of the children had IQs below 85, i.e., were in the "slow learner" range of intelligence.

About 12 percent of the children were classified as having perceptual problems on the basis of poor Bender-Gestalt test scores and results of other tests of visual-motor development. No sex differences were apparent at this age.

About 7 percent of all children had serious language disabilities, i.e., verbal subtest scores that were markedly inferior to nonverbal test scores. Almost all were serious enough to interfere with school achievement. Twice as many boys as girls were classified in this category.

About one-fourth of all the children at this age had some behavior problems; about one child out of every six children had problems severe enough to interfere with school achievement as judged by the panel. More boys than girls were among them. Significant sex differences were apparent among the incidences of "chronic nervous symptoms" and of "restless, distractible" behavior.

Of the children in the time sample for whom any physical defects or health problems were noted, almost three-quarters had problems so minor that they interfered little, if at all, with normal functioning. Most of these were allergies known to be prevalent in Hawaii. About 6 percent of the children were moderately or severely handicapped as a result of physical defects. These included severe congenital defects: spina bifida; atresias of the gastrointestinal, genitourinary, and auditory systems; congenital heart anomalies; cleft lip and palate; cerebral palsy, and developmental defects of the central nervous system. Also included were defects involving vision (1.6 percent), and hearing (1.1 percent); and the presence of hernia; hydrocele, persistent thyroglossal duct, pilonidal sinus, and orthopedic problems.

Some of the two-year diagnoses were not confirmed; others changed as a result of treatment. These decreases were more than equalized by additional children whose handicaps had become apparent in the interim or who had acquired handicaps. Handicaps were acquired due to accidents (blindness, epilepsy, orthopedic problems), infections (hearing loss due to chronic otitis media, uveitis, chronic urinary tract infection, tuberculosis), or to other causes (Legg-Perthe's disease, Letterer-Siewe syndrome, hemolytic anemia, and severe asthma).

The comparatively minor role of postnatally acquired defects, even by age 10, is shown by the fact that such defects were only half as frequent as handicaps of congential origin: 2.1 percent versus 4.5 percent (French et al. 1968).

Services Needed

Although the interdisciplinary panel estimated that only 7 percent of the 10-year-olds in the time sample would continue to need special medical care, they agreed that the need for special educational help was over five times as great—39 percent. By far the most pressing need was for remedial help in the basic skills, e.g., reading, arithmetic, grammar, and spelling (32 percent); a smaller group (7 percent) required placement in special classes for children with serious learning disabilities and for the educationally handicapped.

Fortunately, of the 32 percent, over half (18 percent) needed only short-term assistance, which might be provided, at least in part, by volunteer ·tutors and by teachers' aids. This left 21 percent with the most serious problems who were in need of long-term special educational services.

Twice the number of children had serious emotional problems interfering with school progress as the number needing special medical care.

Considering the overlap in these two types of needs, we estimated that almost one-third of all Kauai's 10-year-olds needed long-term educational services or mental health services or both.

Low-Birth-Weight Babies

A grim prognosis for "prematures" is often suggested, particularly in the popular media, with the implication that, if there were no "prematures," much of the mental retardation problem would vanish.

There is no denying the high mortality of the very smallest infants. For example, in our study, only 45 percent of those weighing 1,500 grams or less were alive at 10 years compared with about 90 percent for those weighing 1,501–2,500 grams and born before term gestation, 95 percent for those weighing 1,501–2,500 grams and born at term, and 97 percent and 99 percent respectively of babies over 2,500 grams born before and at term. But it is important to remember that the 45-percent survival rate affected less than one out of 100 births.

With regard to survivors, evidence from our study does not

indicate that "many" of the low-birth-weight babies are doomed to permanently inadequate lives because of mental retardation. One investigator has reported that as many as half of her surviving premature children were uneducable in regular school (Drillien 1964). But these were the smallest infants (under 1,361 grams or three pounds)—representing but a very small proportion of low-weight births—and, in addition, they were drawn heavily from the lowest socioeconomic class. It will be remembered that less than 1 percent of our babies weighed as little as 1,500 grams. The half who survived to age 10 had weighed 1,300–1,400 grams; three were of 30 weeks gestation (two cesarean sections) and one each of 37- and 38-weeks gestation. The 37-week baby was a microcephalic. One of the 30-week babies suffered from choroidal retinitis, nystagmus, and blindness in one eye; however, with an IQ score of 105 he was performing above average in school at age 10. The remaining three had IQ scores of 94 (two) and 110. At age 10 the latter showed some evidence of a perceptual problem; otherwise, all were progressing satisfactorily.

But for the much larger group of our low-weight babies who had weighed 1,501–2,500 grams at birth, in all respects but one, our 10-year data failed to show that they suffered any significant disadvantages compared to their classmates who had been born heavier. We found no significant difference for total IQ or IQ factor scores, achievement, language, emotional, and physical problems, or any need for special medical, educational, or mental health services. However, children weighing less than 2,500 grams had a significantly higher percentage of perceptual problems compared with those who started out weighing more. Perhaps with the passing of a few more years, this noted excess of perceptual problems may also fail to distinguish our low-birth-weight children.

We also looked at the 10-year outcome of the groups described in chapter 3 as conceived small, true prematures, and the dysmature babies. Perhaps because of the small numbers in the subcategories, and/or the interrelationships of ethnic group and socioeconomic status, we found no significant difference in status judged by the measures used at 10 years of age.

In summary, because the proportion of children who weighed 2,500 grams or less was small, and because these children had physical, learning, and behavioral problems about as frequently as did all others, even if all of our follow-up children had been born heavier, the effect on the 10-year-old picture would have been

TABLE 12   Percentages of Children with Achievement, Learning, Emotional, and Physical Problems at Age 10, by Severity of Perinatal Stress

Type of Problem	Severity of Perinatal Stress				Results of Chi-Square Test
	None N=421	Mild N=233	Moderate N=172	Severe N=36	
School Achievement Problems	**43.7**	**42.5**	**43.0**	**58.3**	$\chi^2 = 3.29$
D or F in reading, writing, or math	41.8	38.2	39.5	38.9	$\chi^2 = 0.77$
One or more grade below CA	10.7	7.7	7.6	16.7	$\chi^2 = 4.28$
In mentally retarded class or institution	1.0	1.7	3.5	16.7	$\chi^2 = 37.59**$
Mental Functioning Problems	**22.6**	**20.2**	**29.1**	**36.1**	$\chi^2 = 7.43$
IQ below 85	9.7	10.7	9.9	30.6	$\chi^2 = 14.91**$
Perceptual problem	12.1	11.2	15.7	16.7	$\chi^2 = 2.50$
Language problem	7.1	4.3	8.2	0.0	$\chi^2 = 5.53$
Emotional Problems	**24.9**	**24.9**	**33.8**	**27.7**	$\chi^2 = 5.34$
Chronic nervous habit	7.9	4.3	9.9	11.2	$\chi^2 = 5.66$
Hyperkinetic symptoms	5.7	4.4	8.1	8.3	$\chi^2 = 3.04$
Persistently withdrawn	8.3	9.1	10.5	2.8	$\chi^2 = 2.37$
Persistently overaggressive	7.1	7.3	6.4	5.6	$\chi^2 = 0.25$
Other emotional problems	3.1	3.5	5.6	2.8	$\chi^2 = 2.72$
Significant Physical Handicap	**5.2**	**4.7**	**7.0**	**22.2**	$\chi^2 = 17.73**$

NOTE: Reprinted, by permission of the American Academy of Pediatrics, from E. E. Werner, J. M. Bierman, F. E. French, K. Simonian, A. Connor, R. S. Smith, and M. Campbell. 1968. Reproductive and environmental casualties: A report on the 10 year follow-up of the children of the Kauai pregnancy study. *Pediatrics* 42: 112–127.
**p <.01

insignificant. Most of the children at 10 who had been born small were indistinguishable from their peers.

LONG-TERM EFFECTS OF PERINATAL COMPLICATIONS

It can be seen in table 12 that the greatest effects of perinatal stress were found in the proportion of children at age 10 who required placement in special classes or institutions, had IQs below 85 (in the slow learner and mentally retarded categories), and had significant physical problems (predominantly defects of the central nervous system and the musculoskeletal system—cretinism, microcephaly, cerebral palsy, epilepsy, and problems with vision and hearing).

There was a significant difference in mean PMA IQs between children who had undergone severe perinatal stress (mean IQ: 97) and those with moderate, little, or no stress (mean IQ: 103). Significant differences between the perinatal stress groups were also found for four PMA factor scores: Verbal Comprehension (V), Reasoning (R), Perceptual Acuity and Speed (P), and Numerical Ability (N). It must be kept in mind, however, that these differences, though statistically significant, amounted to only six–seven points for the extreme groups (severe versus no perinatal complications).

A somewhat higher percentage of children with severe and moderate perinatal complications had "chronic nervous habits" and "hyperkinetic" symptoms than those with mild or no stress, but the differences are not statistically significant.

We found no significant differences between the perinatal stress groups in the percentage of poor grades received in the basic skill subjects and in the percentage of children who had language or perceptual problems, except for those placed in institutions.

We found no differences in group Bender-Gestalt error scores between children *with* and *without* perinatal stress of the same age. Likewise, we found no differences between the perinatal stress groups in the total percentage of behavior problems at age 10.

Discussion

In general, our findings agree with most of the other follow-up studies of children between the ages of seven to 11 with perinatal complications. Differences found between children with and without perinatal complications centered on a small group of survivors of severe perinatal stress. For children with moderate or mild stress, however, the deficits were minimal, and differences between perinatal stress groups found earlier had become attenuated.

Corah et al. (1965), at Washington University, St. Louis, compared 101 children who had been anoxic full-term babies with 134 children of normal birth at age seven years. They found that differences between normals and anoxics which were significant at preschool age were attenuated at school age. These data agree with our own conclusions. The mean IQ of the anoxic group was four points lower than the normal control group, and anoxics scored significantly lower than the normal controls on the WISC vocabulary test, a test of perceptual-motor functioning, and a test of reading accuracy. A greater number of anoxic children were rated as maladjusted by their parents and were considered by psychiatrists and psychologists to be more impulsive, distractible, and ineffective in communication. They also showed greater impairment on the Vineland Social Maturity Scale.

Schachter and Apgar (1959), at Columbia University, studied a group of 60 children with histories of perinatal complications and 96 normal control children at age eight. They found a five-point difference in mean WISC IQ between the children with perinatal complications and the control group, and a tendency to do more poorly on a test of concept formation and perceptual-motor tests.

Benaron et al. (1960), at Chicago, reported a greater incidence of Stanford-Binet IQs of 70 or less, of abnormal electroencephalograms, and of infantile habits among 30 severely apneic children at age 10, matched with a control group of the same age, sex, race, and low socioeconomic status.

Fraser and Wilks (1959), at Aberdeen, Scotland, studied 100 children with asphyxia and compared them with normal controls between ages seven and 11. They found significant differences in tests of perceptual and motor development between the anoxic and control children and a greater incidence of neurological deficits, including epileptic seizures.

We conclude, therefore, that perinatal complications are related to physical and cognitive deficits at school age, but that such deficits are reasonably minimal for all but the most severely stressed group.

Our findings strongly support an admonition made by Corah et al. (1965, p. 31) in their discussion of their seven-year follow-up: "Some caution must be employed in generalizing from these findings . . . of differences between anoxics and normals . . . when it is possible for such effects to be relegated to a secondary position by environmental forces."

EFFECTS OF QUALITY OF HOME ENVIRONMENT

In our study independent ratings of each environmental factor showed significant associations with outcomes at age 10, except for major physical handicaps. Table 13 presents the findings.

Socioeconomic Status

Socioeconomic status showed a significant association with achievement, intellectual, and emotional problems (persistent aggressiveness) among 10-year-olds on Kauai. The relationship between these outcomes and SES, however, was not as pronounced as the association with the other environmental ratings— educational stimulation and emotional support in the home.

As in the two-year follow-up, socioeconomic status did not differentiate among children with major physical handicaps. The lack of a consistently unfavorable effect due to low socioeconomic status may be explained by the fact that low financial means did not bar Kauai parents and children from access to excellent low-cost medical and public health facilities.

Educational Stimulation

The educational stimulation received in the home was the best criterion to differentiate between children with and without achievement problems, IQs below 85, language, and perceptual problems. Of the children on Kauai whose homes were rated "high" or "very high" in educational stimulation (on the basis of opportunities provided for enlarging the child's vocabulary, availability of books, intellectual leisure-time activities, and encouragement of disciplined work habits), only 14 percent (nine children) had achievement problems in school. In contrast to this, 62 percent (276) of the children in whose homes few or none of these opportunities were available had difficulties with the basic skill subjects in school. Only 21 of the 378 children who had poor grades or were in special classes came from the group with severe perinatal complications.

Only about 2 percent (three) of the children from homes rated "high" and "very high" in educational stimulation had IQs below 85, in contrast to 18 percent (80) of the children from homes with "low" and "very low" educational stimulation. Only 11 of the 94 children with IQs below 85 had undergone severe perinatal stress.

Only 1.5 percent (two) of the children from homes with "high" and "very high" educational stimulation had language problems, in contrast to 9 percent (40) of the children coming from homes with "low" and "very low" educational stimulation.

TABLE 13   Percentages of Children with Achievement, Learning, Emotional, and Physical Problems at Age 10, by Three Environmental Variables

Type of Problem	Socioeconomic Status			
	Above Average N=83	Average N=297	Below Average N=482	Chi-Square Test
School Achievement Problems	19.3	32.0	55.4	$\chi^2=62.34$**
D or F in reading, writing, or math	18.1	30.3	50.2	$\chi^2=48.54$**
One or more grades below CA	2.4	5.4	13.3	$\chi^2=18.41$**
In MR educable or trainable class	1.2	1.3	3.1	$\chi^2=3.03$
Learning Problems	14.5	16.8	29.7	$\chi^2=20.58$**
IQ below 85	3.6	6.4	15.2	$\chi^2=19.02$**
Perceptual problem	7.2	10.1	15.4	$\chi^2=6.76$*
Language problem	3.6	3.4	8.5	$\chi^2=9.09$*
Emotional Problems	14.5	23.9	30.9	$\chi^2=11.32$**
Chronic nervous habits	4.8	7.4	7.9	$\chi^2=.91$
Hyperkinetic symptoms	7.2	5.0	6.2	$\chi^2=.69$
Persistently withdrawn	4.8	7.1	10.4	$\chi^2=4.13$
Persistently overaggressive	2.4	4.7	9.1	$\chi^2=8.16$*
Significant Physical Handicaps	4.8	5.7	6.7	$\chi^2=.56$

NOTE: Reprinted, by permission of the American Academy of Pediatrics, from E. E. Werner, J. M. Bierman, F. E. French, K. Simonian, A. Connor, R. S. Smith, and M.
*p $<$ .05   **p $<$ .01

Among children from homes rated "low" and "very low" in educational stimulation, the proportion of perceptual problems was more than twice as high (17 percent) as among those coming from homes with "high" and "very high" educational ratings (7.5 percent).

The majority of children with serious language problems (40 of 54) and the majority of children with perceptual problems (75 of 110) came from homes rated "low" and "very low" in educational stimulation.

Emotional Support

Ratings of emotional support in the home differentiated better than the other environmental ratings between children with and without behavior problems at age 10.

Educational Stimulation				Emotional Support			
Above Average N=133	Average N=218	Below Average N=488	Chi-Square Test	Above Average N=219	Average N=332	Below Average N=311	Chi-Square Test
14.3	29.5	61.6	$\chi^2=126.19^{**}$	30.6	37.6	59.8	$\chi^2\,51.59^{**}$
12.0	28.5	56.0	$\chi^2=104.66^{**}$	27.8	36.4	53.0	$\chi^2=36.32^{**}$
0.0	3.6	16.1	$\chi^2=47.50^{**}$	4.6	6.0	16.7	$\chi^2=29.30^{**}$
2.2	.4	3.6	$\chi^2=7.88^{*}$	1.8	.3	4.8	$\chi^2=14.80^{**}$
9.8	15.3	33.3	$\chi^2=46.78^{**}$	16.0	20.2	33.1	$\chi^2=23.97^{**}$
2.3	3.9	18.1	$\chi^2=47.02^{**}$	4.6	6.6	20.3	$\chi^2=42.33^{**}$
7.5	8.9	16.7	$\chi^2=13.04^{**}$	10.5	12.0	15.1	$\chi^2=2.59$
1.5	4.3	8.9	$\chi^2=12.28^{**}$	3.2	5.1	9.6	$\chi^2=10.10^{**}$
14.3	22.8	33.3	$\chi^2=22.01^{**}$	13.2	20.5	43.4	$\chi^2=70.07^{**}$
6.8	7.1	7.8	$\chi^2=.18$	2.7	8.4	9.6	$\chi^2=9.48^{**}$
3.0	4.3	7.8	$\chi^2=6.13^{**}$	3.2	5.7	8.0	$\chi^2=5.32$
5.3	8.9	9.6	$\chi^2=2.33$	7.3	4.2	14.5	$\chi^2=21.60^{**}$
1.5	3.2	10.9	$\chi^2=22.73^{**}$	.9	3.6	14.8	$\chi^2=46.82^{**}$
6.0	4.3	7.4	$\chi^2=2.87$	5.5	5.1	7.7	$\chi^2=2.10$

Campbell. 1968. Reproductive and environmental casualties: A report on the 10 year follow-up of the children of the Kauai pregnancy study. *Pediatrics* **42**: 112–127.

About 13 percent (29) of the children from homes rated "high" in emotional support (stable home, both parents present and sharing activities with children, express affection and approval of child, use reasoning for discipline) were judged to have some behavioral problems; less than half of these had problems serious enough to interfere with school achievement. In contrast, 43 percent (135) of the children from homes with "low" emotional support had some behavior problems, and two-thirds of these children had problems serious enough to interfere with school achievement.

The majority of all children with emotional problems grew up in an unfavorable home environment between 2–10 years. Only 10 of the 231 children with behavior problems came from the group with the most serious perinatal complications.

TABLE 14   Means and Standard Deviations of 10-Year PMA IQ for Three Environmental Variables, by Severity of Perinatal Stress

| | Severity of Perinatal Stress | | | | | | | | Results of Statistical Test[a] | |
| | None N=421 | | Mild N=233 | | Moderate N=172 | | Severe N=36 | | | |
Environmental Variable	X̄	SD	X̄	SD	X̄	SD	X̄	SD		
Socioeconomic Status										
High	112	(11)	113	(12)	114	(11)	110	(1)	SxP	F= 0.21
Medium	108	(12)	106	(13)	105	(12)	101	(13)	P	F= 2.03
Low	99	(11)	100	(11)	99	(12)	94	(14)	S	F=26.04**
Educational Stimulation										
High	115	(10)	114	(10)	112	(12)	114	(7)	EDxP	F= 0.65
Medium	105	(11)	109	(11)	106	(11)	106	(7)	P	F= 0.87
Low	98	(11)	98	(11)	97	(12)	92	(13)	ED	F=49.22**
Emotional Support										
High	108	(12)	107	(11)	105	(12)	100	(13)	EMxP	F= 1.76
Medium	105	(11)	106	(12)	105	(11)	104	(10)	P	F= 6.67**
Low	98	(11)	99	(12)	97	(15)	86	(11)	EM	F=28.04**

NOTE: Reprinted, by permission of the American Academy of Pediatrics, from E. E. Werner, J. M. Bierman, F. E. French, K. Simonian, A. Connor, R. S. Smith, and M. Campbell. 1968. Reproductive and environmental casualties: A report on the 10 year follow-up of the children of the Kauai pregnancy study. *Pediatrics* 42: 112–127.
[a]Symbols used to designate variables: (S) socioeconomic status, (ED) educational stimulation, and (P) perinatal stress.
   **p < .01

RELATIONSHIP OF PERINATAL STRESS
AND ENVIRONMENTAL FACTORS TO PMA IQ

When we look at the PMA IQ distribution by both degree of perinatal stress and amount of educational stimulation, it is quite apparent that the difference in mean IQs between children growing up in the most and least favorable home environments from 2–10 years was much larger than that between children from the most and least severely stressed perinatal groups (table 14).

At age 10, perinatal stress accounted for much less of the variance in PMA IQ scores than the quality of the home environment. The effect of environmental deprivation was much more powerful at 10 years than was apparent at age 20 months, even with the children who had no perinatal complications.

For example, at age 20 months we found only a four-point difference in mean Cattell IQ between children from the least and most favorably rated environments who were free of perinatal complications. At age 10, the differences in mean PMA IQ scores between these groups was 17 points on the educational stimulation rating.

The children with severe perinatal stress who had grown up in homes rated "high" in educational stimulation did not differ from children without perinatal stress who were raised in homes favorable to educational stimulation. Both groups achieved mean PMA IQ scores well above the average at 10 years. Much larger was the mean difference between PMA IQs of children with severe perinatal stress coming from homes rated "high" in educational stimulation compared with children with severe perinatal stress coming from homes rated "low."

The relationship between the "emotional support" ratings of the home and intelligence test scores of the children, though positive, was not as strong as the association between educational stimulation in the home and intelligence test scores. Similar findings have been reported from the Fels longitudinal studies (Sontag, Baker, and Nelson 1958): Children whose IQs increased from preschool- to school-age were less dependent upon the mother for emotional support, but had mothers who stressed acceleration and rewarded achievement efforts.

CONCLUSIONS

From the results of our analysis, we conclude that our concern with a continuum of "reproductive casualties" needs to be complemented by a much greater concern with the "environmental casualties" among the young. The children of school age on Kauai who suffered most were not the children who had endured perinatal complications, but the children of *The Other America* about which Michael Harrington wrote so movingly (1962).

The gradient of retarded physical, intellectual, and social development that appeared by age two with increased severity of perinatal complications was pretty much "washed out" by age 10, except for a residue of the most severely stressed children who grew up in unfavorable home environments. The remainder of the children who underwent severe perinatal stress survived the first decade of their lives with amazing resiliency and flourished in homes with adequate educational stimulation and emotional support.

The study children who contributed the overwhelming proportion of school failures, stunted intellectual growth, and emotional immaturity had little or no perinatal stress but had to cope with a world lacking in material opportunities, intellectual stimulation, or emotional support.

We are aware of the need for caution in the use and interpretation of environmental ratings. However, our results are consistent with the findings of several investigators from the United States and Great Britain (Kent and Davis 1957, Kagen and Freeman 1963, Bayley and Schaefer 1964, Honzik 1967) that demonstrated the short- and long-term effects of parental concern and stimulation on children's cognitive development and achievement, and the importance of early parental stimulation of language skills in the child.

In a study of 118 eight-year-olds in Great Britain, Kent and Davis (1957) found that children from homes with unconcerned parents had significantly lower Stanford-Binet and WISC IQs than did children from demanding homes. The unconcerned parents in this English study made few demands on their children, were content if their children merely kept out of trouble, were haphazard and inconsistent in their use of punishment, and gave little encouragement or guidance. Demanding parents set high standards for their children and provided a stimulating home environment with many learning opportunities. Intelligence quotients of the eight-year-old children of demanding parents averaged 124, and of unconcerned parents 97. A difference of more than 20 IQ points has also been noted in Kauai between children from homes rated "high" and those rated "low" in educational stimulation.

Moore (1968) presented similar findings from a longitudinal study of 76 London children, followed from six months to eight years. When social class was held constant, the variables most closely associated with measures of ability, vocabulary, and reading skill at school age were the toys, books, and experiences available to the child, the example and encouragement to speak, and the emotional atmosphere of the home.

Our results with the 10-year-olds on Kauai are also consistent with findings by Dave (1963) and Wolf (1964) who interviewed mothers of 60 fifth grade children living near Chicago. Wolf reported a high correlation (.69) between ratings of the quality of home environment and the children's IQ scores. The strongest factors affecting the children's IQs were found to be the parents' intellectual expectations for the child, the opportunities provided for enlarging the child's vocabulary, the extent to which parents created situations for learning in the home, and the amount of assistance given in learning situations. Dave, using the same interview schedule, reported an even higher correlation (.80) between these environmental ratings and fifth grade achievement scores. As in our study, the educational stimulation ratings of the home were found to correlate more closely with children's IQs and achievement than did measures of parental socioeconomic status, education, and ability.

The Chicago and London studies, as well as our own on Kauai, were done within a normal range of home environments rather than in extreme conditions. In such a setting a general index of social or economic status seems to be a less sensitive indicator of the qualities of the home which have lasting effect on children's cognitive and affective development than the stimulation and emotional support provided by the parents.

In sum, the gap between the development of children with perinatal damage and their normal age peers narrowed between birth and middle childhood. No doubt the more general awareness of physical handicaps and their importance, resulting in an effective crippled children's program, together with progress in medicine, have contributed to this happy result. But the gap between normal children born into poor homes and those in good homes became wider with each year, as evidenced by IQ scores, school achievement, basic communication skills, and emotional and social development.

By the age of 10, nearly one-third of the children in Kauai were having trouble in coping with some aspect of their school environment or had personal problems and were judged to be in need of remedial education, mental health services, or medical care. That this unhappy situation must be largely the result of influences in the environment in which they are growing up is suggested by the fact that 90 percent of the school failures had no record of any perinatal problems. They were normal at birth as far as it was possible to judge.

Of course it cannot be assumed that all children have the same genetic potential for intellectual, emotional, or physical development, but, for its own good, society has the responsibility to give each child an opportunity to achieve his potential. This is clearly not being done. A large proportion of the children having problems as 10-year-olds were born into families in which the parents had little education or little interest in their children's learning, had unresolved emotional problems of their own, and were unable to provide emotional security for their children. A poor home environment might provide minimal food and shelter, but it does not provide for the basic needs of the young child for educational stimulation and emotional security.

CHAPTER 8

Summaries of
Illustrative Cases

IN THIS CHAPTER we contrast the family characteristics and the developmental status of four groups of children at two and 10 years of age. Group 1 consists of 20 children who suffered no perinatal complications and who grew up in a very favorable home environment. Group 2 is composed of 14 children who suffered severe perinatal stress but who grew up in a favorable postnatal environment. Group 3 consists of 29 children without perinatal complications who grew up in a family environment rated unfavorable. Group 4 is composed of 22 children who were exposed to both severe perinatal stress and an unfavorable home environment. Case summaries for all four groups are given in appendix 4.

TWO-YEAR STATUS

The Cattell IQs at two years for group 1 (no perinatal stress and favorable home environment) ranged from 137 (superior) to 88 (low average); no child in this group had a score of more than one standard deviation below the mean.

The range of Cattell IQs for children in group 2 (severe perinatal stress, but favorable postnatal environment) was from average to low average (105–86); one child with severe anoxia did not participate in the first follow-up, but was tested when entering school, and received a Stanford-Binet IQ score of 138.

Children in group 3 (no perinatal stress, but unfavorable home environment) had Cattell IQs ranging from 112 to 74. More than one-half of these children scored below IQ 90, in the "slow learner" range. The range of Cattell IQs in group 4 (severe perinatal stress and unfavorable home environment) was from 89 to 20. All children in this group had "below average" Cattell IQs and four of the children had already been identified as mentally retarded.

77

A similar contrast between these groups emerges from the findings of the independent pediatric examinations. The children in group 1 without perinatal stress who lived in a favorable environment were rated, with only one ("low normal") exception, either superior or normal in physical status. Pediatric examinations showed few handicaps and health problems among the children who survived severe perinatal stress and grew up in a favorable postnatal environment (group 2). Only one child in this group, prematurely born, was considered "physically retarded" at the time of the two-year follow-up.

Of the children without perinatal stress who had grown up in an unfavorable home environment (group 3) nearly one-third had ratings of "low normal" physical status, lowered vitality, and malaise, malnourishment, and evidence of physical neglect. With one exception (a 46-week postmature infant) all of the children who had been exposed to both severe perinatal stress and an unfavorable home environment (group 4) were rated "below normal" in physical status. In this group, one child was diagnosed as a cretin, and one had a diagnosis of microcephaly and spastic quadriplegia by age two.

The two groups of children who grew up in an early environment rated favorable (groups 1 and 3) were more often described as "determined," "persevering," "sociable," "friendly," "independent," "active," "energetic," "responsive," characteristics that are more extroverted and adjusted. This was true both for the children with and without perinatal stress.

In contrast, the two groups of children who had grown up in a family environment rated unfavorable (groups 2 and 4) were more often described as "bashful," "shy," "slow," "fearful," "dependent," "solemn," "uncommunicative." These introverted, maladjusted characteristics occurred more often among children who had also undergone severe perinatal stress.

FAMILY CHARACTERISTICS

The adjectives most commonly used to describe early maternal behavior (postpartum, one- and two-year interviews) for mothers in groups 1 and 2 were "kind," "affectionate," "temperate," "intelligent," "skillful," "responsible," "relaxed," "takes matters in stride," "stable," "good-humored," "contented," "patient," "concerned," "energetic." The most frequently used adjectives to describe the behavior of mothers in groups 3 and 4 were "careless," "childlike," "easygoing," "indifferent," "unintelligent," "irresponsible," "erratic."

The family milieu of groups 3 and 4 represents a striking contrast to the middle-class characteristics of groups 1 and 2 (small families with two or three children; parents high school or college graduate; economic stability, security, and affection). It is replete with social deprivation, isolation, adverse childrearing practices, neglect, and separation experiences.

Many of the breadwinners in the homes rated low in educational stimulation and emotional support lacked adequate education (most had less than sixth grade education; some of the older immigrant parents had received no formal education whatsoever), and they worked in predominantly unskilled or semiskilled jobs on the plantations, in the canneries, in construction work. They were frequently unemployed, and the majority of the families had to rely on some welfare support. Homes were crowded (the average number of children was seven, the maximum number 14), and inhabited by several generations. Frequently one of the natural parents, usually the father, was absent; many mothers had borne out-of-wedlock children by several fathers, had been unmarried at the time of the child's birth, or had lived in common-law marriages. The children had several caretakers in their early years, often slightly older siblings, and there was marital discord, alcoholism, and often marked emotional disturbance or psychiatric illness in one or both of the natural parents.

It is quite apparent that the environment of the children whose families were rated low in socioeconomic status, family stability, and maternal ability provided minimum opportunities for the learning of cognitive and language skills and had already given the very young child maximal opportunities to learn self-defeating techniques, i.e., expectancies of failure and belief in his own worthlessness (McCandless 1965).

Wortis et al. (1963) concluded a recent report on their 2½-year follow-up of lower-class prematurely born Negro children in a Brooklyn ghetto with a poignant statement that is equally valid for the part-Hawaiian, Filipino, and Puerto Rican children in the rural shacks of Kauai:

Many elements in the environment were preparing the child to take over a lower class role. The inadequate incomes, crowded homes, lack of consistent family ties, the mother's depression and helplessness in her own situation, were as important as her child-rearing practices in influencing the child's development and preparing him for an adult role. It was for us a sobering experience to watch a large group of newborn infants, plastic human beings of unknown potential, and to observe over a short span of years, their social preparation to enter the class of the least skilled, least educated and most rejected in our society. [P. 307]

CHANGES IN DEVELOPMENTAL STATUS FROM TWO TO 10 YEARS

The case summaries also illustrate characteristic changes in developmental status from two to 10 years for the four groups of children, representing the favorable and the unfavorable ratings on the "environmental quality" and "perinatal stress" dimensions.

Group 1, the children without perinatal stress who grew up in homes rated favorable in environmental stimulation and emotional support, had 10-year IQs in the superior (128) to average (101) range. No child had achievement problems in school, and all except one had gained IQ points since the two-year follow-up—an average gain of 13 points, with a range from 2 to 28 points.

Group 2, the children who had suffered severe perinatal stress but grew up in homes rated favorable in educational stimulation and emotional support, had 10-year IQs ranging from 125 to 96, from the superior to the average range. One-fourth of these children had some achievement problems, but the overwhelming majority functioned adequately in school. One-sixth had significant physical problems. All children on whom Cattell test scores were available had gained an average of 13 IQ points, an increase similar to the group without perinatal stress which was exposed to a favorable environment.

Group 3, the children without perinatal complications who grew up in homes rated unfavorable in educational stimulation and emotional support, had 10-year IQs ranging from 123 to 70. More than half of these children had IQs below 85, in the "slow learner" or "educable mentally retarded" range. Intelligence quotient point changes from two to 10 years were erratic, ranging from +37 to −20, with an average loss of four IQ points. With one exception, all of the children in this group had serious achievement problems in school; four-fifths also had behavior problems. Nearly two-thirds of the children had verbal subtest scores significantly lower than performance test scores, indicating a serious language disability. Only two children had significant physical defects.

Group 4, the children who had suffered severe perinatal stress and also grew up in homes rated unfavorable, had a very wide range of IQs at age 10, from 117 to 30. One-half of the children in this group were either "slow learners" or mentally retarded;

four-fifths had serious achievement problems; one-fourth had serious behavior problems; and one-fourth had perceptual problems. All but three of the children who had Cattell test scores reported a loss in IQ points since the two-year follow-up. One-third had significant physical defects of the central nervous and the musculoskeletal systems.

The following excerpts from several family interviews when the children were age 10 illustrate characteristic differences in the parents' intellectual expectations for the child, the opportunities provided for enlarging the child's vocabulary, the extent of assistance and facilities provided for learning, the adult models available for identification, the quality of interpersonal relationships, and discipline in the home. Regardless of degree of perinatal stress (severe complications versus no complications), the effect of educational stimulation and emotional support in the home is reflected in the cognitive development, achievement, and behavior of the children. The excerpts describe children from each ethnic group on the island (Anglo-Caucasian, Portuguese, Japanese, Chinese, Filipino, Puerto Rican, Hawaiian and part-Hawaiian, Japanese-Filipino mixtures). Each of the groups (high-low perinatal stress; favorable-unfavorable home environment) is represented by a boy and a girl.

Code No.: 2181-1. No perinatal stress; favorable home environment. Girl; older of two children.

Early environment. Father and mother both professional people and employed; both parents college graduates. Mother rated in one-year interview as "intelligent, resourceful, good-humored, stable, responsible, energetic, outgoing, reasonably relaxed, warm-hearted, affectionate, happy, considerate, permissive, self-controlled, calm, patient"; in two-year follow-up as "kind, temperate, mature, contented, takes matters in stride, easygoing."

Child's status at two years. Physical development superior. Cattell IQ 89. Vineland SQ 110. Child rated "bashful, deliberate, determined, quiet."

Excerpts from family interview at age 10. Both mother and father read to the girl often before she entered school (as early as age two), and she loves to read on her own. Both parents like to read and have broad reading interests. English is the only language spoken at home; the children rarely speak pidgin and its use is discouraged. The girl has a great variety of interests. She takes piano lessons; plays the violin; takes tennis lessons, and loves to play cards, especially bridge. She has her own room with a desk where she usually does her homework and she has won a Top Student Award. The parents discuss daughter's schoolwork during the year when she works on projects and during report-card time; mother attends parent-teacher conferences and father is active in PTA meetings. In spite of the fact that the mother works, the family does a lot of things together: they play tennis and bridge, and go on beach outings, picnics, and dinners. "Whatever we do and whenever we do things, we try to do them as a family." The child loves to chat with her parents about school and whatever is on her mind. The mother considers her very loving and generous, and parents let her know that they are pleased when she is thoughtful. They praise her when she brings her report card home. The mother finds her an easy child to manage, but thinks she very definitely has a mind of her own. Both parents reason with her; mother explains to her what and why something must be done; sometimes they withhold privileges, but usually this is not necessary. She likes people and has friends at school, but is more mature than most of her classmates, and younger children do not interest her as much as older people.

Child's status at 10 years. PMA IQ 117. B+ to A average in basic skill subjects; no achievement, intellectual, or emotional problems. Prepubertal nontoxic goiter, not interfering with school progress.

Code No.: 0175-2. No perinatal stress; favorable home environment. Boy; youngest of four children.

Early environment. Father business manager; two years of college education. Mother high school graduate with two years secretarial school; rated in one-year interview as "intelligent, skillful, good-humored, stable, responsible, outgoing, self-confident, affectionate, happy, permissive," in two-year interview as "kind, temperate, mature, takes matters in stride."

Child's status at two years. Physical development normal. Cattell IQ 108. Vineland SQ 142. Child rated "agreeable, independent, responsive."

Excerpts from family interview at age 10. Mother and father both read books to the child when he was little; he was fascinated by them and now reads a great deal on his own. Mother's reading is extensive and she has a wide range of interests; father's reading is in business and current affairs. English is the only language spoken at home; pidgin is discouraged. The boy has a great many interests: 4H, Boy Scouts, French and Spanish lessons, stamp and coin collections. Both parents are much interested in his school-work; child has certain regular responsibilities: he feeds the household pets, washes the car once a week, cleans the patio and garage. The family does many things together: they golf, water-ski, swim, hike, go horseback riding; mother works with her son on crossword puzzles and likes to read with him; father works with him on arithmetic problems. He talks with both parents a lot; "has a mind that won't quit"; is very curious. Parents are very pleased with him and his schoolwork; mother says "he has been a joy since he was born." They consider themselves a very affectionate family and express it openly; father even more so than mother. Parents never disagree in front of the child; they discipline him by reasoning and occasionally by withholding privileges, but they find he usually does what they tell him to do if he knows why.

Child's status at 10 years. PMA IQ 128. A's in reading and arithmetic; B in grammar and spelling. No emotional or physical problems.

_____

Code No.: 2133-1. Severe perinatal stress; favorable home environment. Boy; younger of two children.

Perinatal conditions. Severe asphyxia; 15 minutes to first breath; mouth-to-mouth and oxygen resuscitation; cyanotic when feeding; lethargic, cried only when stimulated.

Early environment. Father mill official; both parents college-educated. Mother rated in one-year interview as "active, cooperative, pleasant, handles child with confidence."

Child's status at two years. No pediatric or psychologic examinations.

Child's status at school entrance. Stanford-Binet IQ 138.

Excerpts from family interview at age 10. Parents speak no foreign language at home and discourage speaking of pidgin among the boys. Mother read books to the child long before he entered kindergarten. He enjoys reading and reads a book about every two weeks in addition to two children's magazines. Both parents read a great deal. Both husband and wife discuss the boy's schoolwork and his exam papers with him and give him responsibilities around the house for chores. In spite of frequent moves of the family in line with father's work, child has managed to make new friends easily in each community and to adjust well. He has been given the opportunity to be outdoors, to study birds, and to observe his father's work. The family does many things together: deep-sea fishing, hiking, looking for artifacts, sharing yardwork, going to dinner, and playing golf. The boy also likes to hunt with his father. The mother says, "We have nothing to hide from our children." Both parents express their pleasure and approval. They find him easy to discipline. They reason with him and explain to him why they have to set limits. Occasionally they withhold a privilege but never need to use physical forms of discipline. The boy has several friends his own age and gets along well with adults. He is in the Boy Scouts, raises pigeons, and is interested in so many things (archeology, oceanography, science) that his mother remarks, "He never gets bored."

Child's status at 10 years. WISC Full IQ 122. Verbal IQ 125. Performance IQ 114. Bender-Gestalt error score: 9. Child of superior intelligence, with a slight perceptual problem, who is somewhat of an underachiever in school (C average in basic skill subjects). "Very active."

———

Code No.: 1967-1. Severe perinatal stress; favorable home environment. Girl; older of two children.

Perinatal conditions. 35 hours labor without progress; R.O.T. [head in right occipital transverse position]; attempted rotation; cesarean section; blood transfusion; slightly jaundiced infant.

Early environment. Father craftsman; both parents are high school graduates. Mother rated in one-year interview as "relaxed, affectionate, self-controlled"; in two-year follow-up as "affectionate, slightly overprotective."

Child's status at two years. Physical development normal. Cattell IQ 95. Vineland SQ 105. Child rated as "somewhat hesitant, inclined to turn to mother for help."

Excerpts from family interview at age 10. Parents speak only English at home. Pidgin is used occasionally by the children, but the parents, especially mother, try to discourage it. The mother has read books to the girl from the time she was two years old, and the child "loves them." Her father takes her to the library frequently and during school she borrows books from the school library. The father is quite a reader. He is enrolled in extension courses in college. Both parents attend parent-teacher conferences and discuss them later with their children. They are very satisfied with the girl's schoolwork. The family likes to go on outings. The girl talks to her mother about her schoolwork and her day's activities and the parents are proud of her special aptitude in art. When they are pleased with the child, they tell her so and praise her. They discipline her by explaining things to her and sometimes by withholding privileges. "So far we have had no trouble—she is easy," remarks her mother, but she feels that the girl is "emotional." The family doctor attributes periodic outbursts of rash over her body to her emotional sensitivity. She has several friends her own age and likes to be with adults, but has no special interests and hobbies aside from art.

Child's status at 10 years. PMA IQ 122. B average in all basic skill subjects. Regarded by her teacher as "somewhat withdrawn and shy." No physical problems.

Code No.: 1085-2. No perinatal stress; unfavorable home environment. Boy; ninth child.

Early environment. Father farm laborer; has no formal education. Mother has fifth-grade education, was diagnosed mentally retarded. Has had several illegitimate children; is neglectful of her children; leaves ill-kempt house, gambles. Family has welfare assistance—aid to dependent children (ADC). Two older siblings have severe emotional problems requiring community intervention. Mother on rare occasions has violent temper and homicidal impulses. Rated in one-year interview as "careless, indifferent, unintelligent, childlike, irresponsible, erratic, easily angered, impatient"; rated in two-year follow-up as "easygoing, careless, childlike."

Child's status at two years. Physical development normal. Cattell IQ 100. Vineland SQ 113. Psychologist comments on extreme lack of stimulation in child's background and anticipates progressive retardation.

Excerpts from family interview at age 10. Family speaks pidgin English and a foreign language. Neither of the parents can read and there are no books, magazines, or newspapers in the home. No one read to the boy before he entered school, but he likes to read and borrows four or five books every other week from the library. He is in the Boy Scouts and likes it very much. He does his homework any place he can find some quiet; nobody helps him or is interested, though father wants all the children to get a high school diploma so "no be like us." The family never does anything together as pastime and the boy and his mother share no interests. He helps his father with chores occasionally. He does not talk much to either mother or father and his only friends are a neighbor family at whose home he watches television and plays with the younger children. Mother finds him a difficult child to manage; she claims he has a bad temper and hits his sister. Mother "licks him" when he does not come after she has yelled four or five times. She describes the child as a "troublemaker," ever since he started school. When he was a baby he hit his head on the floor when he was angry, but now he hits his brothers and sisters. Mother cannot understand him.

Child's status at 10 years. WISC Full IQ 108. Verbal IQ 125. Performance IQ 87. Bright, imaginative youngster who underachieves in school; Ds in all basic skill subjects. Has chronic nervous habits (stammers, twitches), bullies younger children, acts out problems; fine motor coordination is poor; has perceptual problem.

Code No.: 1857-3. No perinatal stress; unfavorable home environment. Girl; thirteenth child.

Early environment. Father unskilled laborer; periodically unemployed and hospitalized because of chronic illness; has no formal education. Mother has second-grade education; works on nightshifts during the summer in pineapple cannery while older daughters take care of the child. Family gets welfare support (ADC) during periods of unemployment. Mother rated in one-year interview as "good-humored, happy, indulgent, easygoing, indifferent, childlike"; in two-year follow-up as "matter-of-fact, takes matters in stride, easygoing."

Child's status at two years. Physical development normal. Cattell IQ 86. Vineland SQ 105.

Excerpts from family interview at age 10. Both parents foreign-born; speak a dialect and pidgin English at home. Neither parent can read, but older sisters started to read to the girl before she entered school, and she now borrows two or three books each week from the school library. There are no books, newspapers, or magazines in the home, and the child does her homework at a table in the yard. Older sisters help her occasionally with her homework. The girl likes to play with the boys (football, volleyball), and the mother considers her a tomboy. The family occasionally goes to parties or a movie together; mother and daughter occasionally do housework together, but the mother mostly lets her play. The girl tells her mother sometimes about her problems when she gets scolded, but does not talk very much with her father. The mother is pleased when she helps her brothers clean the yard and when she keeps her company; she sends her to buy pastry or candy to let her know that she is pleased or she lets her play. She has no friends outside her large family. Mother is the disciplinarian: "I give her licking or yell."

Child's status at 10 years. WISC Full IQ 123. Verbal IQ 119. Performance IQ 124. C in reading; Ds in grammar, spelling, and arithmetic. Teacher considers her "not motivated, insecure, lacks self-confidence.

Code No.: 0891-3. No perinatal stress; unfavorable home environment. Boy; fourth of nine children.

Early environment. Father unskilled laborer; both parents eighth-grade education. Mother rated in one-year interview as "easygoing, careless, indifferent, lazy, childlike, suggestible, irresponsible."

Child's status at two years. Physical development normal. Cattell IQ 79. Vineland SQ 104.

Excerpts from family interview at age 10. Father has worked sporadically; laid off three–four months this year; now works as a day laborer. Mother works full time since child started school. No one took care of the children; they shifted for themselves. Several children must share a room and sleep together. Family speaks only pidgin English and no one reads to the child; there are no books in the home; parents read only little. The boy has no outside activities, interests, hobbies; he wanted to join the Boy Scouts, but "we can't afford it"; he wants to go to camp, but the father says no. He does his homework in the kitchen, and parents seem not interested in his schoolwork. Mother has never gone to school to

88

talk to his teachers; the children tell her what happens. He cleans the yard and helps his mother in her business. There are no children his age in the neighborhood. The family does little together. Occasionally they go to a wrestling match. The father does not want to go anyplace with the children, and he pays no attention to the boy. The mother says that she and her husband do not fight, but she does not bother him and enjoys other company. Her worries at present are mostly financial; she gets angry at her husband because he does not care whether the children get medical care. He spends the money drinking. "Is bad influence to my kids." The parents never talk about the handling of the children; "We only talk about medical bills, but we don't agree about that." She tells the boy "nice" when he does something well, but his father never lets him know whether he is pleased with him. If he does not mind, she scolds the boy and spanks him occasionally or does not allow him to go swimming or playing. The mother notices that he gets unhappy easily, especially if no one pays any attention to him. He gets angry then and throws things or sulks, "likes to be alone."

Child's status at 10 years. PMA IQ 83. WISC Full IQ 76. Raven's Progressive Matrices IQ 105. Child is in class for educable mentally retarded; Ds in reading and math; Fs in grammar and spelling. Persistently withdrawn and shy; teacher reports he is so quiet she hardly knows he is in the room; will do all his work as best he can.

Code No.: 0401-1. No perinatal stress; unfavorable home environment. Girl; oldest of six children.

Early environment. Mother 16 years old at time of pregnancy; eighth-grade education; father laborer, most of the time unemployed and receiving welfare support. Mother comes from broken home. Frequent domestic upheavals, including separations. Mother seeks help from community agencies to force support from or reunion with husband. Mother rated a poor housekeeper and poor manager of children; described as "unintelligent, dependent, childlike, suggestible, erratic."

Child's status at two years. No pediatric or psychologic examinations.

Child's status at school entrance. Physical development excellent. WISC Full IQ 78. Verbal IQ 71. Performance IQ 90.

Excerpts from family interview at age 10. Father works occasionally, but most of the time unemployed and on welfare. He can
only sign his name, and cannot read. Family speaks only pidgin
English at home and with the children. No one read to the girl.
"She hates reading." There are no books, magazines, or newspapers in the house and neither mother nor father reads or has any
outside interests. The child has no outside activities or hobbies;
she has frequently run away from home. She has no friends of her
own age. "No one comes here." The family does nothing together.
Husband does the shopping most of the time, does not give the
mother money, and does not buy what the children need. He
frequents bars. The mother leaves home when father gets mad. She
would like to get away for good, but does not know how. There is
much quarreling when the husband is at home. Occasionally the
girl talks to her mother about her father and how badly he treats
them. "Better we get another father," the children say, according
to the mother. The mother cannot think of anything that pleases
her about the girl. "She doesn't do what I like to have her do, she
just wants to play." She has no regular chores. "She hates doing
house jobs, only play." Her husband does not bother with the girl,
but the mother finds her a difficult child to manage: "That one
has a hard head. Doesn't want to be told to do things. Grumbles."
The mother says she has to spank her often because the child
answers back. The child gets mad quickly and her feelings are
easily hurt, especially when she quarrels with her younger siblings;
she gets very unhappy and depressed when her parents argue,
which is often. Her mother considers her contrary and stubborn,
thinks that she lies a lot and destroys things on purpose when she
gets mad.

Child's status at 10 years. WISC Full IQ 80. Verbal IQ 69.
Performance IQ 97. Child repeated first and fifth grades; Ds in
reading and math; Fs in grammar and spelling. She is frequently
absent without sufficient reason. When motivated in class, she will
respond and try to produce. However, there appears to be no help
given at home and no encouragement. She is sensitive to criticism
and teasing, will not go in front of the class to recite. Her
Rorschach shows considerable unrelieved tension and aggression;
much of her fantasy involves getting away from home.

_____

Code No.: 0958-1. Severe perinatal stress; unfavorable home
environment. Boy; second of seven children.

Perinatal conditions. Placenta abruptio; profuse bleeding; prolapsed cord; breech extraction; newborn anoxic; resuscitation with oxygen for three–four minutes; gestational age: 37 weeks; weight: 3 pounds 7 ounces; placed in incubator.

Early environment. Father unskilled laborer with sporadic work record and frequent periods of unemployment; multiple-problem family supported by welfare and receiving help of Department of Social Services. Parents married after birth of this child. Father has fourth-grade education; mother has ninth-grade education, but mental age of nine-year-old. Mother was operated on for brain tumor at age 14; hospitalized several times for psychotic reactions and postpartum psychoses. One grandparent also diagnosed psychotic. Family lives with grandparents in poorly furnished home. Much family discord. Mother rated in one-year interview as "indifferent, unintelligent, restless, demanding." Boy taken care of mostly by grandparents whose relationship with child is rated in two-year follow-up as "matter-of-fact, irritable, punitive."

Child's status at two years. Physical development normal; size of head small for age. Cattell IQ 76. Vineland SQ 96. Child rated "bashful, hesitant, fearful, slow."

Excerpts from family interview at age 10. Family discord and periodic unemployment of father have continued over the years. Mother has severe chronic illness. The child lived with an aunt for a while, at school entrance, but is now home. Paternal grandparents still live in the house, but grandmother complains of mistreatment by her son when he is drunk. Family speaks pidgin English and native dialect. None of the adults read or have read books to the child. Boy has no outside interests or hobbies, except goes to a church camp occasionally. Parents do not supervise his homework and many times he forgets to bring it home or finish it. He takes care of yard, and family occasionally goes to the beach or church together. He sometimes goes fishing with his father. Boy talks to his mother only if something goes wrong; she finds him difficult to manage. His father usually spanks him; his mother yells at him and scolds him to "make him mind."

Child's status at 10 years. PMA IQ 74. Attends "adjustment class" for educationally handicapped children after he repeated second grade and was frequently absent from school. Has Ds in all basic skill subjects. Persistently aggressive, acts out problems. Teacher remarks, "Environmental conditions at home seem to magnify his retardation. He will be below average even with the best conditions."

(His younger sister, also participant in the Kauai Pregnancy Study [case 958-4] was born without perinatal stress. The parents refused the pediatric-psychological exam when the child was age two, but at 10 years she has a PMA IQ of 88, receives Ds in all basic skill subjects, and is rated as "persistently withdrawn and lacking in self-confidence."

———

Code No.: 0055-4. Severe perinatal stress; unfavorable home environment. Girl; third of six children.

Perinatal conditions. Mother suffered severe pre-eclampsis; severe anemia; was "near shock" at delivery; treated with oxygen and blood transfusion; newborn cyanotic.

Early environment. Father unskilled laborer; works off and on; has eighth-grade education. Mother has fourth-grade education, is considered "mentally dull" and unable to care for her children adequately. Multiple-problem family; is on welfare assistance when father is out of work; has moved frequently. Mother rated in one-year interview as "unintelligent, childlike, irresponsible, erratic"; in two-year follow-up as "indifferent, easygoing, careless, child-like." When girl was six months old, she was taken to aged grandmother for care. Housework and care of child done by grandmother's common-law husband, who supports family as farm laborer; he is fond of the girl.

Child's status at two years. Physical development low normal. Cattell IQ 71. Vineland SQ 90. Child rated "awkward, bashful, dependent, dull, fearful." Child seems poorly cared for (scars from bites and trauma; dirty unkempt appearance).

Excerpts from family interview at age 10. Grandmother is now senile and incapacitated. As family situation continued to deterio-rate over the years, the girl was placed in a foster home at age 10. Four siblings in classes for the educable mentally retarded. The child speaks native dialect and pidgin English; no "standard" English was spoken in the home. No one read to her, and she does not know how to read well at age 10½. Her own parents had no books, magazines, or newspapers in the home; her new foster parents read a little, mostly newspapers and popular magazines.

No one cared much about her education during the first ten years of her life because her parents, her grandmother, and her grandmother's common-law husband were illiterate. Her foster parents are interested in her schoolwork and try to help her; they work in the yard together, play games, and she has learned to iron and cook with her foster mother. They are pleased that she listens and does not answer back when they tell her to do something. They find her easy to manage; she usually minds, but has to be scolded at times. She cleans the garage and the house, picks up the rubbish, takes care of the garbage, and washes dishes. She now has some friends of her own age (there were no children around to play with at her grandmother's home), and a former foster mother whom she likes.

Child's status at 10 years. PMA IQ 69. Attends class for the educable mentally retarded. Ds in reading, arithmetic, writing, and spelling. No evidence of any neurological or physical abnormalities. No emotional problems.

CHAPTER 9

The Predictive Value of Early Pediatric and Psychological Examinations

THROUGHOUT THE DISCUSSION of our follow-up studies in the preschool and school years, we have emphasized the need for early identification of those children who suffer from serious physical and psychological handicaps associated with poor birth histories and/or a deprived environment. In this chapter we will show how we approached this objective by pooling the resources of two disciplines, pediatrics and psychology, and by making use of existing sources of information in the community.

We were impressed by the great amount of useful information contained in the records of practicing physicians, hospitals, health and social agencies, and the schools. Researchers commonly ignore such sources and expend great amounts of time and money repeating examinations and devising elaborate methods for obtaining data that are already recorded.

A point of special interest was our discovery in the pilot study that we could safely eliminate routine pediatric examinations on all the children at age 10 by making full use of the records of the physicians, the hospitals, the health department, and the schools. It was far less costly and more efficient to utilize existing sources of information than it would have been to repeat every procedure. This enabled us to concentrate on collecting new data in the diagnostic examinations at age 10.

We will focus our discussion on the "batting average" of the two-year pediatric and psychological screening procedures in identifying children who had significant physical handicaps, mental retardation, or achievement problems by age 10.

Our study should be encouraging to those who believe that an important contribution to child health and development can be made by providing every child in the community with at least one complete physical-sensory and psychological examination during early childhood.

93

THE IDENTIFICATION OF PHYSICAL HANDICAPS

Of the study group examined at age two, 72 of the 77 children identified as having significant congenital defects were available for follow-up at age 10; of these, 29 had been severely handicapped and 43 moderately handicapped. Their status at age 10 is discussed below.

Children Severely Handicapped at Age Two

This group of children consisted of (a) 21 with serious physical-sensory defects without evidence of mental retardation, and (b) eight children with significant physical defects and mental retardation.

Physical-sensory defects without mental retardation at age two. Defects included were spina bifida, atresias of the gastrointestinal, genitourinary, and auditory systems, congenital heart disease, congenital deafness, cleft lip and palate, and cerebral palsy.

Of the original group of 21 children, 17 diagnoses were confirmed at age 10 and four-fifths of the confirmed cases were still severely handicapped. All had received extensive specialized medical care, mostly under the auspices of the crippled children's program, and required continuing special care. Some surgery was still in progress. Not surprisingly, half of this group by age 10 had developed additional defects not manifest or not detected at age two (convulsive disorders, hearing defects, and vision defects). One child, with Sturge-Weber syndrome, had a 10-year IQ of 55, and was attending a special class for the mentally retarded. The other 20 were in regular school, but only half were progressing satisfactorily.

Physical-sensory defects with mental retardation at age two. These eight children were multiply handicapped with developmental defects of the central nervous system, congenital endocrinop-athies, or congenital deafness and blindness, and were severely mentally retarded as well. At age two their IQ scores ranged from 16 to 61 (median under 20).

By age 10, all previous diagnoses were confirmed. All these children had received extensive diagnostic and treatment services, mostly under the Crippled Children's program, and all still required care. Half of these children had additional physical defects which had not been found at age two (severe visual and hearing problems and epilepsy). All but one had an IQ below 60 (median under 40) and were in special schools or institutions for the mentally retarded.

Children with Less Severe Defects at Age Two

This group consisted of 43 children, half of whom had suspected strabismus; the remainder had cases of hernia, persistent thyroglossal duct, pilonidal sinus, or orthopedic defects.

By age 10 eye problems had been diagnosed for less than half of the previously suspected strabismus cases. The overdiagnosis may have been due, in part, to the difficulty of detecting strabismus in Oriental children. All had received diagnostic examinations and treatment services (corrective lenses, surgery) where recommended. Most of the children with confirmed early strabismus were still visually handicapped despite treatment. All those with other types of defects had received recommended care (principally surgery), and none of the children suffered from more than a mild residual defect.

School achievement for these children differed little from achievement for the total study group.

Additional Physical Handicaps at Age 10

In reviewing the status of 10-year-olds in the 1955 cohort who, at age two, were called defect-free, we found 14 children with congenital defects not noted by two years and 16 with acquired defects.

Children with congenital handicaps not evident at age two. Of these 14 children, one had mild spastic quadriplegia diagnosed at six years, and one had multiple endocrinopathy diagnosed at eight years. An additional 12 children were moderately handicapped. Nine of these had eye problems, and failure of early diagnosis and treatment probably resulted in more handicapping than would have been necessary. Two others had developed epilepsy and one an orthopedic defect. All will continue to need specialist care periodically.

Children with acquired defects. Sixteen children without abnormalities at age two had acquired handicaps due to accidents (blindness of one eye, epilepsy, orthopedic defects), infections (hearing loss due to chronic otitis media, uveitis, chronic urinary tract infections, tuberculosis) and other causes (Legg-Perthe's disease, Letterer-Siewe syndrome, hemolytic anemia, severe asthma). Urological investigations failed to reveal congenital anomalies in the three children with chronic urinary-tract disease. The panel considered that only the three children with organic epilepsy, hemolytic anemia, and Letterer-Siewe's disease were severely handicapped. None of the children were mentally retarded.

A point needing emphasis is the high "batting average" of the pediatrician-psychologist screening procedures in identifying significant congenital defects with and without mental retardation at two years. We want to stress the fact that the procedures used were *screening* procedures, not thorough diagnostic examinations which would not have been feasible for large-scale application.

The principal weakness was in connection with eye problems. In view of the importance of early detection of children with serious vision problems, greater attention should have been placed in these early examinations on special sensory screening procedures.

THE PREDICTION OF INTELLIGENCE AND ACHIEVEMENT AT AGE 10

Early studies of mental development with normal and superior children from middle-class homes concluded that infant tests were limited as predictors of later intelligence (Bayley 1949). Recently, however, both psychologists and pediatricians have suggested that the predictive usefulness of infant tests may be improved if clinical ratings are combined with objective test scores, and that future performance may be more readily predicted for less able children than for average and superior groups.

Oppenheimer and Kessler (1963) commented on the continuing dialogue between pediatricians and psychologists about the value of giving intelligence tests to young children. They point out that, among practitioners in the child-care professions, there is "either an attitude of total reverence for the IQ or an attitude of skepticism." In their review they cite a number of historical developments and research findings by both groups which may have contributed to the expressed differences of opinion.

The pediatricians' assessment of the intelligence of the Kauai children correlated only moderately (.32) with test scores.* On the basis of a follow-up of a sample of 60 children assessed as "below normal" at school age (five–eight years), it was concluded that prognosis was poor for children assessed as below normal by

---

*The median age at the time of the pediatric examination was 19½ months and that for the psychological examination was 20 months, with 95 percent of the children examined before age two. For convenience, they are referred to as the two-year examinations.

both methods, and that a low test score should not be discounted, even if the pediatrician thought the child was "all right" (Bierman et al. 1964).

We present here our findings of the predictive value of the two-year pediatric and psychological examinations in forecasting intelligence and achievement at age 10.

Table 15 shows that the two-year Cattell IQ was the best single predictor of IQ at age 10 and of achievement level in middle childhood. For the total group, the correlation was moderate (.40 for PMA IQ, .49 if the individual IQ scores on the WISC are included, and .44 for achievement level).

Pediatricians' clinical ratings of the child's intelligence level at two years did not correlate as highly as the other predictors (test scores, parental SES, and education) with IQ and achievement level at 10 years (.19 for PMA IQ, .30 for the "best" IQ, and .24 for achievement level).

When we combined Cattell IQ with all other information available at the time of the two-year follow-up (parental education, occupation, Vineland SQ, pediatricians' clinical appraisal, and perinatal stress score), we obtained slightly higher multiple correlations (R of .50 for PMA IQ, and .58 for highest IQ). Most of the added predictive power was contributed by parental socioeconomic status; this variable, added to the Cattell IQ, significantly raised the correlation with PMA IQ at age 10 (from .40 to .49, and the correlation of highest IQ from .49 to .56).

The addition of the Vineland Social Maturity Scale and the pediatricians' appraisal of intelligence did not significantly add to the predictive power of the Cattell Infant Intelligence Test.

Our correlations, for the whole range of intelligence, agree more with the findings of other longitudinal studies (Honzik 1948; Bayley 1949; Cavanaugh et al. 1957) between the ages of 20 months and 10 years than with the high correlations (.84) reported by Knobloch and Pasamanick (1966) between 4–12 month Gesell DQs and 6–10 year Stanford-Binet IQs.

However, for the children at the lower end of the IQ distribution, predictions for both the Cattell IQ and the pediatricians' clinical appraisal of intelligence are better. The results here came close to those reported by Knobloch and Pasamanick.

The correlation between Cattell IQ and highest IQ (usually a WISC) at 10 years for the 36 children (23 boys, 13 girls) who scored below 80 at age 20 months was significantly higher than that for the total group (.71). This difference is statistically

TABLE 15 Predictions of Ten-Year IQ and School Achievement from Infant Examinations and Family Variables at Two Years

	10-year Measures					
	PMA IQ[a]		Highest IQ		School Achievement	
Predictors	Boys N=310	Girls N=326	Boys N=312	Girls N=327	Boys N=312	Girls N=327
	r^b	r	r	r	r	r
Perinatal Stress Score	-.03	-.07	-.08	-.09	-.02	-.09
Pediatrician's Rating of Intelligence at 19 Months	.23	.13	.33	.26	.26	.19
Cattell IQ at 20 Months	.35	.45	.46	.51	.42	.44
Psychologist's Rating of Intelligence at 20 Months	.34	.35	.43	.40	.38	.32
Vineland SQ at 20 Months	.18	.18	.31	.26	.27	.27
Socioeconomic Status	.37	.34	.38	.34	.29	.22
Father's Education	.42	.33	.40	.30	.30	.24
Mother's Education	.37	.29	.37	.29	.31	.16

NOTE: Reprinted, by permission of the University of Chicago Press and the Society for Research in Child Development, from E. E. Werner, M. P. Honzik, and R. S. Smith. 1968. Prediction of intelligence and achievement at 10 years from 20 months pediatric and psychologic examinations. *Child Development* 39: 1063–1075.
[a]Three retarded children did not take a PMA test.
[b]r .18 p < .001; r .15 p < .01; r .13 p < .05.

98

significant. The pediatricians' clinical ratings correlated .76 with highest IQ at age 10 for these children. A combination of Cattell IQ and pediatricians' ratings yielded the highest correlation with 10-year IQ (R of .80). The addition of the perinatal score, the Vineland SQ, and parental socioeconomic status did not improve our predictions for this group.

Although knowledge of parental socioeconomic status improved the prediction of school-age intelligence from tests at two years for the whole range of intelligence, *the combination of pediatricians' appraisal and Cattell IQ was the most powerful predictor of later intellectual status of children with Cattell IQs below 80.*

The agreement between the Cattell IQ at 20 months and independent ratings by the pediatricians was much closer for the less able children (.72) than for the total study group (.32).

Psychologists' and Pediatricians' Ratings of Intellectual Status at Age Two and Achievement Problems at Age 10

Each of the three children rated "defective" and three-fourths of the 96 children rated "below average" in intellectual status by the psychologists at two years had achievement problems at 10 years. The predictive validity of the pediatricians' clinical appraisal of the children's intelligence (made independently) was about the same: three-fourths of the 32 children whom they designated as "low normal" and three of the four children labelled "retarded" by the pediatricians later had serious problems in school. The pediatricians' clinical ratings, however, identified fewer children than the psychologists' appraisals and predicted more successfully for boys than girls.

Cattell IQs and School Achievement Problems at Age 10

Fourteen of the 15 children who scored more than two SD below the mean on the Cattell Infant Intelligence Test at two years had problems in school at 10 years. Forty percent of these children were in special classes or institutions for the mentally retarded, 20 percent in grades below chronological age; the other children in this group were receiving grades of D and F in the basic skill subjects (reading, arithmetic, grammar, spelling).

For the 56 children whose Cattell IQs at two years were between one and two SD below the mean, predictions for 10 years were also fairly impressive. Three-fourths had problems in school. Only a small percentage (two children) were in special classes, but nearly one-third were in grades below chronological age, and more than 40 percent had grades of D and F in basic skill subjects.

Status at Age 10 of the Children Who Were Rated "Below Normal" in Intelligence by the Pediatricians and Had Cattell IQ Scores Less Than 80 at Age Two

This group contains nine boys and three girls. The pediatricians considered all 12 children to be slow in their speech development, 10 to be of low physical status, and seven to be atypical in their motor development.

At age 10, only one child of the 12 was functioning normally, with a PMA IQ of 97 and no achievement problem in school. His psychological examination during the first follow-up was not considered optimal because of the presence of a visitor.

Four of the 12 children were in special classes and two in training centers for the mentally retarded; one additional child was eligible for a class for the educable mentally retarded. Four children had IQs in the "slow learner" range (80–85) and were considered in need of long-term remedial education, because they were failing in basic skill subjects, especially reading. In sum, *the prognosis remained poor for the children who were considered "below normal" in early childhood by both pediatricians and psychologists.*

Status at Age 10 of the Children Who Were Rated "Normal" in Intelligence by the Pediatricians, but Had Cattell Scores below 80 at Age Two

Of the 24 children (14 boys, 10 girls) who were rated by the pediatrician as having "normal" intelligence, though their Cattell IQs were below 80, 21, or 83 percent, had problems in school. Twelve had IQs below 89, i.e., in the "slow learner" range, and three were eligible for classes for the educable mentally retarded. Ten had repeated a grade sometime between kindergarten and third grade. One child, though of average intelligence, had an extremely poor Bender-Gestalt score and was considered in need of long-term mental health services.

Of the three remaining children without school achievement problems at age 10, two had incomplete Cattell tests, and the other was rated by the psychologists as lacking in "verbal responsiveness" on the infant test. In sum, *prognosis was poor for children who scored below 80 on the Cattell test at age two, if their examination was considered adequate, regardless of the pediatricians' estimate of intelligence.*

Status at Age 10 of Children Who Were Rated "Below Normal" in Intelligence by the Pediatricians, but Had Cattell Scores of 80 or Higher at Two Years

These 24 children (14 boys and 10 girls) had IQs ranging from 81 to 107 at two years, but the physicians rated them "below normal" in intelligence. Seventeen of these children had physical deficits, 15 were poor in speech development. Ten were of both poor physical status and slow in talking. One child had congenital heart disease. Of the remaining children who were rated normal physically and seemed normal in speech development, the pediatrician observed "little spontaneous activity," "hyperactive reflexes," and "mother not too bright."

At the time of the 10-year follow-up, 14 of the 24 children needed some remedial help. Two had IQs of 73 at 10 years and were eligible for special classes for the mentally retarded. Their Cattell IQs at two years were 83 and 86 respectively. Five children had IQs in the "slow learner" range (81–89) at age 10. Three were also retarded in visual-motor development as reflected by poor Bender-Gestalt scores and four had repeated the first grade. Among this group, pediatricians had noted "small size" in two of the boys, "malnourishment" in two other boys, and "hyperactivity" in a child who was considered in need of placement in a special class for the educationally handicapped.

In sum, *pediatrician's recognition of slow physical development in early childhood is helpful in detecting the child who, though of normal intelligence, is retarded in his visual-motor development and has difficulty in acquiring reading skills.*

DISCUSSION

It should be stressed that in our study the assessment of intellectual potential was made *independently* by pediatricians and psychologists. It is apparent that the predictive value of infant examinations could have been increased if the psychologists and pediatricians had combined their impressions and arrived at a joint diagnosis, particularly for the children whom either profession assessed as below normal.

The impressive facts that emerge at age 10 are that (*a*) when both disciplines agree on the status of the young child, prediction is good, and (*b*) an infant test score that is low should not be discounted by the pediatrician even if the child appears normal in his physical development. Each method, the pediatricians' and the psychologists' appraisals, selects some "low" cases and potential "failures," and, in a doubtful diagnosis, the added information provided by the other discipline may add considerably to the accuracy of the prognosis.

Low scores on infant tests and low ratings by pediatricians of intelligence and developmental status at age 20 months correctly identified those children who had limited ability and achievement level at 10 years. In addition, low parental socioeconomic and educational status were characteristic of those children whose intelligence level declined from "normal" to "borderline" intelligence and educational retardation in the interval from 20 months to 10 years.

In summary, *a combination of retarded development and deprived environment in infancy is more predictive of serious achievement problems at school age than either infant examinations or family variables alone.*

CHAPTER 10

Ethnic Differences

WITH THE EXCEPTION of a rather extensive literature on Negro-Caucasian differences and some reports on American Indian children, few studies of child health and development have dealt with children in the United States who are non-Caucasian and descend from non-Western cultures (Anastasi 1958). Children on Kauai are predominantly of Oriental and Polynesian descent, and so the opportunity is offered to study ethnic differences in subcultures where little cross-cultural research has been done so far.

Although three-fourths of the 30,000 inhabitants of Kauai were born in Hawaii, the population has a varied ethnic background, with the Caucasians in a minority. Of all the live births occurring in 1955, for example, 33 percent were of Japanese descent, 23 percent Hawaiian and part-Hawaiian, 18 percent Filipino, 6 percent Portuguese—descendents of immigrants from the Azores— and only 3 percent Anglo-Caucasian. The remaining 17 percent were principally mixtures of ethnic groups other than Hawaiian, mostly children of Japanese-Filipino marriages.

The Anglo-Caucasian minority contributes a higher percentage of professional, proprietary, and managerial positions in the plantation society than any other ethnic group on the island, but the Japanese represent the majority of the middle class on Kauai. They are the only other ethnic group that has a sizeable number of professional, managerial, and business men. The Portuguese are concentrated in the working class, largely in the skilled trades and among technically trained people. The part- and full-Hawaiians and the Filipinos make up the bulk of the semiskilled and unskilled workers on the plantations.

In the following section we will present data that illustrate ethnic differences found in two major areas of investigation: (a) infant mortality rates, and (b) differences in measures of ability and achievement among preschool- and school-age children. Ecological factors in the community and family environment that are associated with these differences will be discussed, with special emphasis on those factors that appear helpful in intervention programs designed to raise the general level of health care and educational achievement.

ETHNIC GROUP DIFFERENCES IN INFANT MORTALITY RATE AND RELATED ECOLOGICAL FACTORS

Hawaii offers unique opportunities for the researcher to study associations between a number of environmental factors and a child's chances of survival. It is possible in these islands to make comparisons between racially and genetically similar population groups from Asia—the one remaining in the agricultural setting of their homeland, the other, migrants, exposed to an environment undergoing rapid industrialization and urbanization.

The two largest immigrant population groups on Kauai are the Japanese and the Filipino, whose descendents make up about two-thirds of the population of the island. The residents classified as Japanese are largely the children and grandchildren of the young agricultural workers recruited to work on the plantations in the late 1800s and early 1900s. They came mostly from the southern prefectures of Yamaguchi, Hiroshima, and Kumamoto, and from Okinawa (Lind 1946). The Filipinos, whose immigration took place mainly in the 1920s and 1930s, came principally from the agricultural districts of northern Luzon and from some of the southern islands (Philippines 1946).

Lind aptly says in his book *Hawaii's People* (1967), "Certainly the plantation sponsors of the mass migrations which brought more than 400,000 persons to Hawaii from all parts of the earth during the past century had little awareness of the social forces which they were setting in motion." In the early days of these immigrations there was certainly nothing to suggest that by the midcentury these people would form a large part of a group which had achieved levels of living and health among the best in the world.

A downward trend in infant mortality has been observed during the past fifty years in every region and country of the world from which reasonably accurate data are available, but the rates of decline differ markedly. Probably the most dramatic reductions of all have taken place in Hawaii. For this reason, and because comparable data are more readily available, we have analyzed the effects of rapid and radical changes in the environment on the infant mortality rate of the Japanese and Filipino immigrant groups to Hawaii, and have made comparisons, as far as possible, with similar populations in Japan and the Philippines, and with the native Hawaiian population (figure 5).

As recently as 1906, the reported infant mortality rate of almost 400 per 1,000 live births in Honolulu and 240 in other parts of the Islands reflected social and economic conditions in Hawaii which must have been among the worst in the world. These rates were as high or higher than those reported around that period from India, Ceylon, Mexico, and Chile (Chandrasekhar 1959).

In contrast, during the early 1900s in Japan, the infant mortality level of 152 for the country as a whole was considerably lower than in Hawaii (Japan 1960). Rates by prefectures of major migration were reported to be even lower, ranging from 100 to 135 per 1,000 live births. The Japanese immigrants thus came from an environment more favorable to the health of their infants than Hawaii offered at that time.

A part of the cultural heritage of the Japanese immigrants must have been the ability to adapt their values quickly to their new environment, because as early as 1924 the infant mortality rate among the Japanese residents in Hawaii was well below that of the territory as a whole, 88, as compared to 100 (Lind 1967).

By 1916, when migration to Hawaii from the Philippines was beginning, infant mortality rates reported from the provinces of major migration ranged from 120 to 170 and were as high as 400 per 1,000 live births in Manila, rates far exceeding those of Japan (Philippines 1921). The rate among the newly arrived Filipinos in Hawaii in 1924 was 262, a reflection of the childbearing and rearing practices of this new immigrant group.

So much for the situation at the time these groups arrived in Hawaii. Now for a look at what has happened since. In the 13 years between 1912 and 1924, the infant mortality rate in Hawaii was reduced from 200 to 100 per 1,000 live births; by 1939 it was cut in half again, and by 1949 it fell again almost a half. The level at midcentury was 25 deaths per 1,000, a decade later (1959) 24 per 1,000. The 1959 infant mortality rate on Kauai was below that of the continental United States (26) and comparable with those of New Zealand, Sweden, and the Netherlands, the countries with the lowest mortality rates in the world.

The Japanese and the Chinese share the lowest rates. The infant mortality rate for the Japanese dropped to 21 by 1959, for the

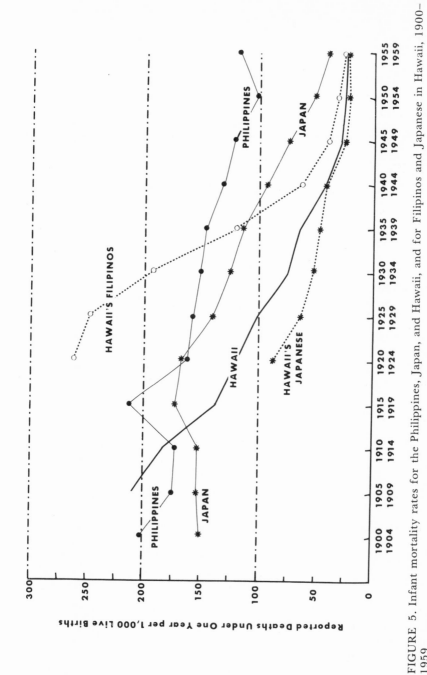

FIGURE 5. Infant mortality rates for the Philippines, Japan, and Hawaii, and for Filipinos and Japanese in Hawaii, 1900–1959

Reprinted, by permission of the publisher, from J. M. Bierman and F. E. French. 1963. Ecological influences on infant mortality among Japanese and Filipino immigrants to Hawaii. *Journal of Tropical Pediatrics and African Child Health* 9:3–13.

Filipinos to 33, and for the Hawaiians and part-Hawaiians to 44 per 1,000 live births (Hawaii 1959).

Since 1924, the infant mortality rate has been reduced by three-quarters in Hawaii and Japan, but by only one-third in the Philippines. Levels were 24 for Hawaii, 34 for Japan (1959), and 109 for the Philippines (1958) (United Nations 1960).

On a time basis, it can be seen that Hawaii attained Japan's present rate about 20 years ago, and that of the Philippines 30 years ago. It is also evident that both the Japanese and Filipino groups in Hawaii shared this improvement. The rates among the Japanese group dropped from 88 in 1924 to 21 in 1959, with an even more spectacular drop for the Filipino group from 262 to 33.

In attempting to analyze some of the reasons for the drop in infant mortality rate in Hawaii, we have reminded ourselves that this spectacular picture is merely one visible result of a complex interplay between environmental stimuli and host responses in a rapidly changing environment. We shall now briefly examine some of the principal ecological factors known to influence the health status of children.

Geographic-Climatic Influences

The areas of the Philippines from which the immigrants came to Hawaii are characterized as having a tropical, wet, monsoon, rain-forest type of climate; southern Japan (from which most Hawaiian migrants came) is classified as being humid and subtropical. The tropical wet climate of the Hawaiian Islands, therefore, was not a great change for either the Filipino or the Japanese immigrant groups. Neither geography nor climate would appear to be the predominant factor in determining the level of infant mortality in the Pacific area. The Maori in New Zealand had a rate of 58; the European population of that country, a rate of 20 (1957). In 1959, the native Hawaiians in the Hawaiian Islands had an infant-mortality rate of 44; the Japanese in Hawaii, a rate of 21 (United Nations 1960).

Housing and Sanitation of the Family Environment

Crowding, lack of sanitary excreta disposal, and availability of water in the home are all related to the prevalence of communicable, respiratory, and enteric diseases that contribute so largely to high infant mortality rates. While over one-third of the infant deaths in both Japan and the Philippines in recent years are reported to be due to these environmental causes, such causes in

108

Hawaii have accounted for only a fifth or less of the deaths for the past several years. Of the live births which we have studied intensively on Kauai, only four of the 32 first-year deaths were due to communicable or infectious diseases.

Although comparable information on the housing of the people in the areas of origin is not available, we are surely safe in assuming that such housing compares unfavorably with that found in the state of Hawaii, where in 1960 only 13 percent of housing units were of two rooms or less, 99 percent were equipped with running water, 96 percent had bathing facilities, and 94 percent had flush toilets. Even excluding the metropolitan area of Honolulu, 94 percent of units used water from a public or private system (United States 1960).

Because uncrowded housing and sanitation in the immediate environment of the infant are crucial factors in determining infant mortality, we must conclude that the improvements experienced by the Japanese and Filipino immigrants contributed substantially to decreasing the risks for their infants.

Nutrition

Nutritional deficiencies play an important role in infant mortality in large parts of the world. Beriberi continues to be one of the major public health problems of the Philippines (International Cooperation Administration 1955). In 1955, almost 20,000 infant deaths were attributed to this cause. This disease in Japan, whose rice-eating population also has a beriberi problem, is now on the decline, but as late as 1959, with about the same number of live births as the Philippines, 1,700 infant deaths were reported from this cause (Japan 1960).

In addition to the number of infant deaths caused by specific nutritional deficiencies, other forms of malnutrition such as protein deficiencies (which may be ascribed to enteritis or respiratory diseases), contribute substantially to infant mortality. In Hawaii, nutritional diseases have not been an important factor in infant mortality for the past 30 years.

When one considers the oft-referred-to persistence of cultural dietary habits, it is worthy of note that immigrants to Hawaii made very rapid changes. In the beginning new food habits were imposed on the male laborers who were fed and housed by the plantations. Later, with the arrival of women and the establishment of families, efforts were made to revive old-country habits. However, the importation of food items from the countries of origin was both expensive and inconvenient, so increasingly the new but readily available foods were utilized. With the maturing of the second and third generations, assimilation and acceptance of Western patterns proceeded rapidly (Lind 1967).

The eating habits of the people on Kauai presented a great contrast to the typical rice-vegetable diet of rural Japan and the Philippines. In an intensive dietary study carried out on a sample of pregnant women on Kauai, we were impressed by the wide variety of foods consumed. In addition to typical United States mainland foods, there were Chinese, Japanese, Hawaiian, Portuguese, Filipino, and Italian dishes, used not only by the women with these national backgrounds, but by the others as well (Hueneman, French, and Bierman 1961). There were no meatless diets encountered and most women ate a variety of meats, fish, and poultry. Two-thirds of the protein was, on the average, from animal sources, compared with one-third in Japan. In our study of all pregnant women on Kauai, no nutritional problems were recorded on any of the medical records, except for the few cases of obesity and anemia of pregnancy found in 6 percent of the women.

Medical Care

Among the factors exerting a direct influence on infant mortality is the amount and quality of medical care available to mothers during pregnancy and childbirth and to their infants. Higher maternal and infant mortality rates among low-income groups in most countries are closely related to discrepancies in availability and quality of medical care. Commonly, large cities have modern hospitals and medical centers, while rural areas and small towns have only rudimentary services. This is undoubtedly related to the generally observed lower infant-mortality rates in cities than in rural areas.

It is notable that the plantations in Hawaii began very early to provide medical, nursing, and hospital care for the workers and their families. Before the 1940s these services, as well as housing, were perquisites of employment. Since then a cooperative prepayment system for plantation workers and coverage by insurance plans from other groups has given virtually all pregnant women on Kauai access to prenatal care in a physician's office or dispensary, delivery in a hospital, and medical and hospital care for their infants. Evidence of the good health status from our Kauai study is the fact that 80 percent of the women mentioned no chronic illness during their pregnancy and a very small number of infant deaths were due to preventable causes. This speaks well for the accessibility and quality of medical care, and also reflects preventive services provided by the health department.

Not only has the economy of Hawaii been able to afford good medical facilities and services, but great progress has been made toward providing an equitable distribution among all residents through the plantation medical and voluntary prepayment plans.

Level of Public Health

It is well recognized that Hawaii has long had an outstanding public health program. The story of its progress during the past century is one of the most encouraging chapters in public health history (Lee 1954). During the first two decades of the century the Territorial Board of Health included among its principal activities health examinations of immigrant laborers for the presence of infectious diseases, sanitation of the plantation labor camps, attention to adequate water supplies, proper drainage, sanitary garbage, refuse and excreta disposal, and adequate housing to eliminate overcrowding. There can be no doubt of the effectiveness these traditional public health measures had when concentrated on the new immigrants and their surroundings. Largely these were *direct* methods: vaccination required by law; quarantine, condemnation, and destruction of unsanitary dwellings; campaigns against rats and mosquitos; and drainage of swamps. In this role public health served as the "change agent" for mitigating many environmental hazards, and among the first results to be noted from such measures was a reduction in infant mortality.

The early public health activities affected nearly all alike, whether they liked it or not, and a minimum of effort was required by the people served. But the fact that the native Hawaiian population appeared to benefit the least raises the question of host factors even in connection with such straightforward measures as these. For one thing, during the early 1900s the Hawaiians were just beginning to recover from the effects of devastating epidemics which had threatened them with extinction during the nineteenth century. Furthermore, they tended on their own volition to withdraw into the remote rural areas of the Islands which were more to their liking and way of life, and thus were less accessible to public health measures.

During the past decade the many new public health activities which have been inaugurated in Hawaii have included educational campaigns against specific diseases and accidents, and stress on prevention in the fields of mental health and mental retardation. These campaigns will have to depend much more on the understanding and active cooperation of the population than have previous successful measures of manipulating the environment.

Medical and public health services in Hawaii, as elsewhere, will require an increased understanding of human behavior, whether in combating the remaining infant mortality problem (the deaths due largely to factors which damage the fetus during the prenatal period or premature labor), the congenital defects of large numbers of survivors who are handicapped for life, or the problems of failure in school.

Another challenge is the need for knowledge about factors influencing human fertility and the need to reach some demographic equilibrium to prevent mounting population density. Between 1932 and 1950, the crude fertility rate of the Filipinos dropped from 312 per 1,000 persons to 192 in Hawaii, the fertility rate of the Japanese from 170 to 102, approximating the level of middle- and upper-class Caucasians (Lind 1967). Perhaps the citizens of Japanese origin will provide the leadership for an effective population policy in Hawaii that will maintain high standards of health and living as have the citizens of the Japanese homeland.

Even though increasing income and educational levels of the immigrants, in comparison with their lands of origin, have undoubtedly contributed to the rapid gains made in the survival rate of their children, significant group differences in levels of ability and achievement at preschool- and school-age among children from different subcultures do remain at present on Kauai, leading to different rates of success and failure in education and the acquisition of skills for the future.

ETHNIC GROUP DIFFERENCES IN ABILITIES AND ACHIEVEMENT AT TWO AND 10 YEARS

In the following section we will examine differences at three socioeconomic levels (above average, average, below average) among children from five subcultures on Kauai (Anglo-Caucasian, Japanese, Filipino, Hawaiian and part-Hawaiian, and Portuguese) on measures of achievement and ability at preschool- and school-age. These differences will be discussed in the light of differing childrearing attitudes, language styles, and emphasis on achievement and educational stimulation in the different subcultures.

Differences at Age Two

Vineland Social Quotients. No significant differences were found in social maturity among children from the five ethnic groups and the three socioeconomic levels (table 16). Children of Japanese ancestry, however, had a higher mean social quotient than the children from the other ethnic groups, including the Anglo-Caucasians. The high mean SQs point to the high degree of acculturation that has taken place in Kauai among children whose parents or grandparents came from cultures with quite distinct methods of childrearing, such as the Japanese and Filipino (Whiting 1963). Reports by Sikkema in Hawaii (1947), and by Kitano in Los Angeles (1961) have pointed to the fact that Nisei parents adopt Western customs rapidly and resemble their neighbors much more closely in their behavior than do their own parents who were raised in Japan.

Cattell IQs. Significant ethnic group differences were found on the Cattell Infant Intelligence Scale before age two. The Japanese had the highest mean Cattell IQ (103); the Filipino children had the lowest mean Cattell IQ (95); and Portuguese, Anglo-Caucasians, and Hawaiians occupied an intermediary position with mean Cattell IQs of 99, 98, and 96, respectively.

The superiority of the Japanese preschoolers on the Cattell test was maintained regardless of socioeconomic status. For the other ethnic groups, including the Anglo-Caucasians, there was a direct relationship between mean Cattell IQ scores and socioeconomic status. This was not true for children of Japanese ancestry. Their mean Cattell IQs for the above average, average, and below average SES level were 103, 102, and 103, respectively.

These results may well reflect the early effect of differential parental expectations among the different subcultures. Kitano (1961), using the Parental Attitude Research Inventory for a comparison of childrearing attitudes between the Nisei and their Japan-born parents, found significant differences between the two generations, with the Nisei putting less stress on "fostering dependency" and "excluding outside influences" and more stress on "approval of activity" and "acceleration of development."

While there is a fairly extensive literature on the socialization of Japanese children both in Japan and on the mainland United States (Norbeck and De Vos in Hsu 1960), few references on the socialization of Filipino children could be found. W. F. Nydegger and C. Nydegger have described the way in which a Filipino infant and preschool child is reared in a closely knit community in the Philippines (Whiting 1963). Infancy is characterized by indulgence and constant attention through a pattern of communal child care; few, if any, demands are made on the child. Maturation is seen as a leisurely process, one that adults do not accelerate. There is no specific encouragement to walk, talk, or develop other skills. On Kauai, more Filipino than Japanese children were in extended families with many children and several adults in the home (grandparents, other relatives), while most of the Japanese children lived in small nuclear families.

Differences at Age 10

School achievement problems. Significant differences were found among the ethnic groups in the percentage of school achievement problems at age 10 (table 17). The Anglo-Caucasian and the Japanese children had the smallest percentage of school achievement problems at age 10, about half the proportion of that of the other ethnic groups on Kauai.

For each ethnic group, there was a significant increase in percentage of poor grades as the socioeconomic ladder was descended, but the Japanese consistently had the smallest percentage of achievement problems among the various ethnic groups, no matter whether they came from the above average, average, or below average socioeconomic levels. Even in the lowest SES group, the proportion of achievement problems among the Japanese children was well below that of the other ethnic groups.

The Anglo-Caucasian and Japanese children had the smallest percentage of poor grades in the basic skill subjects; the Hawaiians and the Filipinos had the largest percentage. About one child out of every five Anglo-Caucasian children, and one child out of every four Japanese had Ds or Fs in reading, writing, or arithmetic. Contrasted to this, we found that one child out of every *two* Hawaiian and Filipino children had such problems. Ethnic differences were especially pronounced in reading problems. Two to three times as many children of Hawaiian or Filipino origin had serious reading problems as the Anglo-Caucasian and Japanese children. Differences among the ethnic groups in percentage of poor grades in each basic skill subject were significant.

Significant differences were found among the ethnic groups in the percentage of children placed in a grade below chronological age or placed in special classes for the mentally retarded. Of the ethnic groups other than the Anglo-Caucasians (who had no children in a grade below CA), the Japanese had the smallest percentage of children placed in grades below chronological age (2.4 percent), while the Portuguese had the largest percentage (21.7 percent). The Portuguese also had the largest proportion of children placed in special classes for the mentally retarded or in institutions (8.7 percent). The Anglo-Caucasians on Kauai had no

TABLE 16 Mean Scores and Standard Deviations of Five Ethnic Groups on Tests of Social Maturity and Intelligence

	Ethnic Group													
Age at Follow-up and Tests Administered	Total Study Group (N=635)		Japanese (N=253)		Full- and Part-Hawaiian (N=180)		Filipino (N=138)		Portuguese (N=46)		Anglo-Saxon Caucasian (N=18)		Analysis of Variance F value[a]
	$\bar{X}$	SD	$\bar{X}$	SD	$\bar{X}$	SD	$\bar{X}$	SD	$\bar{X}$	SD	$\bar{X}$	SD	
Two-year Follow-up													
Vineland SQ	117	14	118	13	115	15	115	13	116	12	115	13	1.21
Cattell IQ	99	12	103	12	96	12	95	10	99	12	98	12	3.63**
Ten-year Follow-up													
PMA IQ	103	12	108	12	99	12	101	10	96	12	112	12	7.34**
PMA factor V	102	14	107	13	98	13	98	12	95	12	115	13	6.16**
PMA factor S	101	16	105	16	97	16	99	16	91	13	107	13	5.82**
PMA factor R	106	16	112	14	101	15	104	14	96	17	115	13	6.93**
PMA factor P	102	16	105	16	99	16	100	17	97	18	105	13	1.78
PMA factor N	101	13	106	12	98	12	100	12	96	13	101	10	6.97**

NOTE: Reprinted, by permission of the publisher, from E. E. Werner, K. Simonian, and R. S. Smith. 1968. Ethnic and socioeconomic status differences in abilities and achievement among preschool and school-age children in Hawaii. *Journal of Social Psychology* 75: 43–59.

[a]Two-way analysis of variance for ethnicity and socioeconomic status; F values are for the effect of ethnicity.

**p < .01

TABLE 17   Percentages of Children with Achievement, Perceptual, Language, and Emotional Problems at Age 10, by Ethnic Group

| | Ethnic Group | | | | | |
Type of Problem	Japanese (N=253)	Full- and Part-Hawaiian (N=180)	Filipino (N=138)	Portuguese (N=46)	Anglo-Saxon Caucasian (N=18)	Chi-Square Value
Achievement Problem	27.7	53.9	52.2	52.2	22.2	41.41**
D or F in reading, writing, or math	26.9	49.4	47.1	41.3	22.2	29.25**
One or more grades below CA	2.4	13.9	9.4	21.7	0.0	30.77***
In MR class or institution	.4	2.8	3.6	8.7	0.0	14.49***
Perceptual Problem	8.7	13.3	14.5	13.0	16.7	4.04
Language Problem	3.6	8.9	8.0	6.5	0.0	7.17
Emotional Problem	18.6	27.8	28.3	34.8	27.8	9.51*

NOTE: Reprinted, by permission of the publisher, from E. E. Werner, K. Simonian, and R. S. Smith. 1968. Ethnic and socioeconomic status differences in abilities and achievement among preschool and school-age children in Hawaii. *Journal of Social Psychology* 75: 43–59.

*p < .05
**p < .01

children in special classes or institutions; the Japanese had one child who was mentally retarded at age 10 (0.4 percent), the Hawaiians had 2.8 percent, and the Filipinos 3.6 percent. Differences in the percentage of children placed in special classes were significant for the different ethnic groups.

Language problems. No Anglo-Caucasian child had a language problem, i.e., had verbal subtests markedly inferior to nonverbal subtest scores on the intelligence tests administered at age 10. Of the other ethnic groups, the Japanese had the smallest percentage

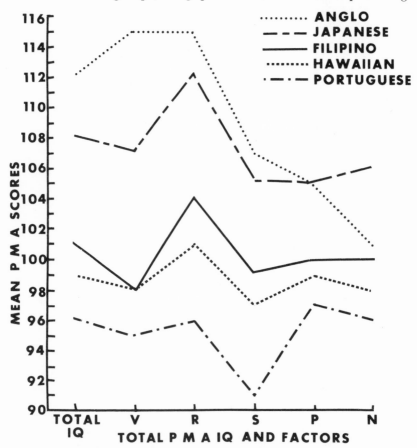

FIGURE 6. Patterns of PMA IQ and factor scores by ethnic groups at age 10
    Reprinted, by permission of the publisher, from E. E. Werner, K. Simonian, and R. S. Smith. 1968. Ethnic and socioeconomic status differences in ability and achievement among preschool and school-age children in Hawaii. *Journal of Social Psychology* 75:43–59.

of language problems (3.6 percent), while the Hawaiians and part-Hawaiians had the largest percentage (9 percent). The differences among the ethnic groups in language problems was too small, however, to reach statistical significance.

Perceptual problems. The Japanese had the smallest percentage of perceptual problems, i.e., poor Bender-Gestalt reproductions or low scores on PMA factor P or S (9 percent). The Anglo-Caucasians had the highest percentage of perceptual problems (17 percent). The differences among the ethnic groups were too small, however, to be statistically significant.

Emotional problems. Significant differences were also found among the ethnic groups in percentages of emotional problems. The children of Japanese ancestry had fewer behavior problems than the other ethnic groups, even less than the Anglo-Caucasians (19 percent versus 28 percent). This was true at every socioeconomic level.

Primary Mental Abilities. Significant differences were found among the different ethnic groups on the total mean PMA IQ and on four out of the five factor scores: Verbal Comprehension (V), Reasoning (R), Space (S), and Numerical Ability (N). Differences among the ethnic groups were not significant for factor P (Perceptual Acuity and Speed). Ethnicity affected both level and pattern of primary mental abilities (figure 6).

The Anglo-Caucasians had the highest mean PMA IQ (112), followed closely by children of Japanese ancestry (mean PMA IQ: 109). The Portuguese children had the lowest mean PMA IQ (96), with the Filipinos, Hawaiians, and part-Hawaiians occupying intermediary positions, having mean PMA IQs of 101 and 99 respectively.

On the verbal comprehension, reasoning, and space factors the same rank order of ethnic groups was found: the Anglo-Caucasians ranked first, the Japanese second, the Filipinos third, the Hawaiians and part-Hawaiians fourth, the Portuguese fifth.

On the perceptual acuity and speed factor, Anglo-Caucasians and Japanese ranked first. On the numerical factor the Japanese ranked first, the Anglo-Caucasians second, followed by the Filipinos, the Hawaiians and part-Hawaiians, and the Portuguese in descending order.

The pattern of Primary Mental Ability factor scores was similar for the Japanese, the Filipinos, and the Hawaiians, with the

Japanese scoring at a considerably higher level. The pattern of Primary Mental Abilities of the Anglo-Caucasians and the Portuguese differed from the other groups and quite markedly from each other. The Anglo-Caucasians scored on a consistently high level, the Portuguese on a lower level of ability.

Socioeconomic level produced marked differences in levels of Primary Mental Abilities, especially in total PMA IQ and in the Verbal Comprehension and Reasoning factors. It did not produce discernible differences in the pattern of abilities between children from below average and average homes. Lower SES children scored about one standard deviation below the mean of the middle-class children on all PMA factor scores, including the factors of space, perceptual acuity and speed, and numerical ability, usually considered to be the least culturally saturated.

Educational Stimulation at Age 10

The Anglo-Caucasians had the highest percentage of "above average" ratings in the educational stimulation provided by the home, followed by the Japanese. This was in contrast to the Portuguese, Filipinos, and Hawaiians, where the majority of homes were rated "below average" in educational stimulation. A higher percentage of Portuguese than Filipinos and Hawaiians were rated as average (37 percent versus 27 percent), but less than 9 percent of the homes in all three groups (Filipino, Hawaiians, Portuguese) were rated "above average." In contrast, the proportion of "above average" ratings among Japanese homes was nearly three times as high as that among Filipino, Hawaiian, and Portuguese homes (25 percent).

Emotional Support at Age 10

Similar, but not quite as pronounced, ethnic group differences were found in ratings of emotional support available in the home, i.e., the presence of opportunities for satisfactory identification with adult models and positive parent-child relationships. Again, the Anglo-Caucasians had the highest percentage of "above average" ratings, followed by the Japanese. The Portuguese occupied an intermediary position. Filipino and Hawaiian homes received the highest percentage of "below average" ratings, but in every ethnic group the majority of the homes were rated as providing at least adequate emotional support.

DISCUSSION

The analysis of ethnic differences among children from five subcultures at three socioeconomic levels on Kauai demonstrates that there are ethnic differences in school achievement and Primary Mental Abilities at age 10 that are independent of socioeconomic status. Ethnic differences were already apparent on infant tests before the children had reached age two.

Our results complement the findings of three other studies of differential patterns of mental abilities in children from different cultural groups and at different ages: Lesser, Fifer, and Clark (1965) found significant differences at age six in verbal, reasoning, spatial, and numerical abilities between middle- and lower-class Jewish, Chinese, Puerto Rican, and Negro children in New York City. Roberts and Robinson (1952) reported differences in patterns of PMA tests for 10-year-old Caucasian and Negro children from two socioeconomic levels in the urban South. Walters (1958) found differences on the PMA between Maori children from several social classes and city children of European descent in New Zealand at ages 11–14.

The Anglo-Caucasian children in Kauai and New Zealand and the Jewish children in New York City were all superior in verbal comprehension. The Japanese children in Kauai, the Maori children in New Zealand, and the Chinese children in New York City all performed well on tests of perceptual acuity, spatial orientation, and numerical ability. In contrast, the Portuguese children on Kauai did as poorly on tasks requiring verbal comprehension and spatial orientation as the Puerto Rican and Negro children in New York City and the urban South.

Differences in patterns of mental abilities among the different ethnic groups in these studies were maintained regardless of socioeconomic status or age. The socioeconomic differences at age 10 that were found in the Kauai study affected only the level of abilities and were similar to differences at age six reported by. Lesser et al. (1965) and at age 13 by Havighurst and Breese (1947). Lower-class children, as a group, were consistently inferior to middle-class children in verbal comprehension, reasoning, space, and numerical ability on the PMA.

Some of the ethnic group differences found in patterns of mental abilities among the five subcultures on Kauai may be explained by variations among the ethnic groups in the reinforcement given to their children for learning different mental skills, as

Lesser et al. have suggested. Some may be due to differences in achievement motivation and the amount of educational stimulation provided in the home. Some may be ascribable to differences in language styles, to the extent to which pidgin English and/or a foreign language is spoken in the home. Differences found on the infant tests between the various ethnic groups may be due to variations in childrearing practices, to the relative emphasis on the acceptance of maturation as a leisurely process not to be hastened or interfered with.

Background data on the children obtained in our study are only suggestive, but we have some evidence from our own and other studies that may begin to explain what factors bring about differences in level and pattern of abilities and achievement.

The Japanese on Kauai, as the Japanese in California and Chicago (Darsie 1926; Strong 1934; Darcy 1953; Norbeck and De Vos 1960) were as a group superior to the other non-Caucasian groups in ability and achievement, and, with the exception of verbal comprehension, equaled or excelled the middle- and upper-class Anglo-Caucasian children. Our data on the amount and type of educational stimulation available in their homes suggest that one of the major reasons for their "good standing" is the fact that in the majority of the Japanese homes emphasis is placed on the value of education, on disciplined work habits, and on respect and esteem for intellectual pursuits, even when the parents have not had much education.

Our data seem to confirm the hypothesis by Caudill and De Vos (1956) that the success of the Japanese immigrants in the process of accommodation and assimilation to a new (Western) culture may be due to the compatibility found between the value system of the culture of Japan (the "Tokugawa" ethic) and the "Protestant" ethic. Both share the values of politeness, respect for authority, duty to community, diligence, emphasis on achievement of long-range goals, and the importance of keeping up appearances.

In contrast to the Anglo-Caucasian and the Japanese homes, about half of the Portuguese and the majority of the Hawaiian and Filipino homes were rated "low" in educational stimulation on the basis of our family interviews. Our results reinforce the popular stereotypes of these groups reported by Norbeck in *Pineapple Town: Hawaii* (1959).

Hawaiian and Filipino children, though ranking in intermediary positions between the Japanese and Anglo-Caucasians and the Portuguese in measures of mental abilities, received the largest percentage of poor grades in the basic skill subjects. This seems to suggest lack of achievement motivation rather than lack of ability. The emphasis on maturation as a leisurely process in infancy that has been reported by the Nydeggers (in Whiting 1963) as characterizing childrearing in the barrios of the Philippines was also reflected in the lower scores Filipino infants received on the Cattell Infant Intelligence Test.

The native Hawaiians seem to suffer from the same handicaps that afflict the American Indians on the mainland: a higher infant mortality rate than the "immigrant populations" and a disadvantage in acquiring the basic skills necessary for economic success in the environment altered by the outsiders.

The Portuguese, in contrast to the other immigrant ethnic groups, have been in the Hawaiian Islands for a longer period of time—nearly a century. Lind, in *Hawaii's People* (1967), points out that, even today, they resemble a peasant immigrant group, slow in upward mobility and somewhat suspicious of those seeking higher education. As a group, the children of Portuguese descent had the poorest showing on tests of ability and had the largest proportion of children in grades below their chronological age and in special classes for the mentally retarded. Many Portuguese children attend parochial schools on the island that do not have special provisions for the slow learner. Their extremely poor showing on tests of spatial functioning was similar to that reported by Porteus on the Maze Test (1965) and to that of many investigations of American Negro children (Anastasi 1958). A similarly poor showing was found by Lesser et al. (1965) among Puerto Rican children in New York. It is interesting to speculate how much a different concept of "time" might contribute to low scores on speeded performance tests among children from these cultures. Lower scores on timed performance-type tests have also been reported in studies of Mexican-American and American Indian children.

All three groups of children, Hawaiian, Filipino, and Portuguese, had below average mean scores on the verbal comprehension factor. Information on the extent to which pidgin and/or a foreign language is spoken in the homes of these children indicates that about four-fifths of the children of Hawaiian and Filipino descent and three-fourths of the children of Portuguese ancestry speak pidgin frequently at home, both with adults and their peers. In addition, two-thirds of the Filipino children grew up in homes in which a Filipino dialect was often spoken.

The effect of poor language models at home has been

demonstrated in the reading problems of these children at school (Werner, Simonian, and Smith 1967). More than 40 percent of the children in whose homes pidgin was spoken had grades of D of F in contrast to 10 percent of the children in whose homes English and a foreign language, but no pidgin, was spoken. The increased proportion of reading problems among children from families speaking pidgin on Kauai existed for each socioeconomic group; families in which pidgin was spoken more frequently had more children with serious reading problems (Fs and/or reading one grade or more below CA). Thus pidgin, with its primitive grammar and word structure, seems to have had a significantly adverse effect on the reading achievement of a sizeable proportion of the Hawaiian, Filipino, and Portuguese children at school.

In our culture, "intelligence" presupposes possession of linguistic skills by which ideas are generated and communicated. A facility in the use of verbal skills greatly enhances the child's ability to solve problems whether they are formulated in verbal or nonverbal terms. The poorer showing of the Filipino, Hawaiian, and Portuguese children on both the verbal and the performance parts of the PMA test is probably affected by the language styles of their homes. Their success or failure in school and the world at large, however, depends on a grasp of the verbal and reasoning skills needed to master an increasingly complex technology. Their test performance, therefore, appears to be a fair measure of their present cultural distance from the Anglo-Caucasian and Japanese groups in their readiness for educational and vocational activities in a developed economy and Western culture.

Early recognition of ethnic group differences in achievement and patterns of abilities may help us to find better ways of diagnosing and preventing educational handicaps among these children. It seems quite apparent from our study that socioeconomic class differences alone do not explain the differences in measured capacity and achievement among children from different subcultures.

Much has been made recently of the plight of the black child, usually an "immigrant" to the city from the rural South, who must confront a white culture with the stigma of racial prejudice and who is tested by culture-biased tests and judged by white middle-class standards. We might gain a little more insight into how we can overcome his plight and the plight of other minority children if we look at members of another ethnic group in white America that have done exceedingly well, regardless of differences in color and physical appearance and regardless of the fact that their ancestors came from the economically depressed, peasant classes of their homeland.

We are speaking here of the Japanese. At every social class level, whether middle class, working class, or lower class, they have fewer achievement, intellectual, and emotional problems than the other ethnic groups. Among other things, their strength seems to lie in the amount of educational stimulation they receive at home. This kind of educational stimulation, and, equally important, good language skills, are teachable and can be transmitted to children of other ethnic groups, if not at home then through special community programs for preschoolers and through compensatory programs in the schools, using teacher aides and volunteer tutors.

In the meantime, we might well ponder the fact that our knowledge of the growth of intelligence is based on a very small sample of humanity, predominantly Caucasian middle-class children, and that the world these children inherit is overwhelmingly nonwhite and has a non-Western cultural heritage. It is time we expand our interdisciplinary efforts to learn more about the cognitive and affective development of the children from cultures other than our own.

CHAPTER 11

Sex Differences in Parent-Child Correlates of Ability

RECENTLY BAYLEY AND SCHAEFER (1964) presented an intriguing hypothesis concerning sex differences in intellectual development. Reporting on longitudinal data from a sample of 26 boys and 27 girls from the Berkeley Growth Study, they noted that the correlations between children's IQs and the parents' estimated IQs is higher for girls. They also found more lasting relationships between early maternal behavior and later developing characteristics for boys, including the child's later IQ. They suggested that the intellectual performance for boys is more responsive to environmental events, while that of the girls has a larger component of genetic control.

In search of additional evidence for this hypothesis of a sex difference in response to environment, Bayley reviewed a series of eight studies (1966) that show higher parent-daughter than parent-son correlations in mental abilities (IQ, education) at ages 2–10 years.

Maccoby, in her review of research on sex differences in intellectual functioning (1966), pointed out that this hypothesis remains to be checked against other bodies of data. Both Kagan and Moss (1959) and Honzik (1957, 1963) found in their longitudinal samples in Ohio and California that, while the correlations between measures of parental ability (education, IQ) and child's IQ develop earlier in the girls, the correlations become significant for the boys by the time of school entrance.

Data from the Fels longitudinal study and the Berkeley Guidance Study also showed a significant relationship between parental behavior and the intellectual development of girls (Crandall et al. 1964; Honzik 1967). Maccoby concluded that existing data do not permit us to either support or reject the Bayley-Schaefer hypothesis unequivocally and that the issue must remain open for further evidence.

During the course of the Kauai study we were able to obtain intelligence test scores for one or both parents of 485 children (231 boys and 254 girls) of the cohort of 1955 births. In addition we have the environmental ratings at ages two and 10 years that reflect the quality of the family environment in which these children grew up. The findings of our study, then, with a considerably larger sample than the Berkeley and Fels longitudinal studies and representing children from all socioeconomic and intelligence levels, should contribute additional evidence on sex differences in parent-child correlates of ability.

Correlations between the Cattell IQs of sons and daughters at two years and measures of parental ability, education, and socioeconomic status are presented in table 18.

Correlations between the PMA and WISC IQs of sons and daughters at 10 years and measures of parental ability, education, and environmental ratings are presented in table 19.

In 8 out of 10 correlations, the IQs of girls at two years on the Cattell Infant Intelligence Scale showed higher relations with measures of parental ability and education than the Cattell IQs of the boys at the same age.

At age 10, in 7 out of 11 sets of correlations, the IQs of the daughters had a higher relation to measures of parental ability (IQ) and the environmental ratings (educational stimulation, socioeconomic status, emotional support) than the IQs of sons. The pattern was the same for parent-child correlates of ability on both group and individual intelligence tests. The difference between the sexes in favor of the girls was significant for all environmental ratings.

However, while the correlations between measures of parental ability (IQ, education) were significant only for the girls at two years, parent-child correlates of ability were significant for both boys and girls at age 10 years.

The findings of our study are in agreement with Honzik's study (1963) at comparable ages. She also reported an earlier appearance of parent-child resemblance for the girls in the Berkeley Guidance Study and noted a continuing increase in parent-son resemblance through middle childhood.

At both ages, two and 10 years, there was a slightly higher correlation between father-daughter IQs than between father-son IQs in the Kauai sample. For the total and the verbal part of the paternal IQ test, this correlation was also higher than the mother-daughter correlates of ability at ages two and 10 years.

The IQ of the son at age 10 correlated slightly higher with

TABLE 18 Correlations between Children's IQs at Two Years and Measures of Parental Ability and Socioeconomic Status

Variables	N Cases		Cattell IQ at Two Years	
	Boys	Girls	Boys	Girls
Father's IQ				
Total	104	96	.13	.29**
Verbal	104	96	.19	.33*
Nonverbal	104	96	.14	.33**
Mother's IQ				
Total	152	165	.05	.19*
Verbal	152	165	.06	.03
Nonverbal	152	165	.09	.26**
Father's Education	171	179	.15	.26**
Mother's Education	179	191	.19*	.21**
Socioeconomic Status	180	192	.23**	.09
Father's Occupation	179	191	.21**	.14**

NOTE: Reprinted, by permission of the American Psychological Association, from E. E. Werner. 1969. Sex differences in correlations between children's IQ's and measures of parental ability and environmental ratings. *Developmental Psychology* 3 (1): 282.

*p < .05
**p < .01

TABLE 19   Correlations between Children's IQs at 10 Years, by Sex, and Measures of Parental Ability and Environmental Ratings

Variables	N Cases		Group Intelligence Test PMA IQ		Individual Intelligence Test Highest IQ	
	Boys	Girls	Boys	Girls	Boys	Girls
Father's IQ						
Total	129	131	.21*	.32**	.24**	.31**
Verbal	129	131	.31**	.40**	.32**	.37**
Nonverbal	129	131	.13	.24**	.04	.22*
Mother's IQ						
Total	196	213	.30**	.28**	.30**	.30**
Verbal	196	213	.29**	.20**	.22**	.21**
Nonverbal	196	213	.32**	.38**	.29**	.36**
Father's Education	219	238	.31**	.31**	.31**	.27**
Mother's Education	225	250	.33**	.28**	.34**	.29**
Educational Stimulation	231	254	.40**	.53**	.37**	.52**
Socioeconomic Status	231	254	.24**	.34**	.23**	.32**
Emotional Support	231	254	.23**	.28**	.21**	.28**

NOTE: Reprinted, by permission of the American Psychological Association, from E. E. Werner. 1969. Sex differences in correlations between children's IQ's and measures of parental ability and environmental ratings. *Developmental Psychology* 3 (1): 283.

*p < .05
**p < .01

the IQ (total and verbal) of the mother and with her education than with the father's IQ. This finding, suggestive of a higher relationship between IQ of child and IQ of the opposite-sex parent, was similar to the one reported by Honzik (1963) and by Bing (1963) in a study of child-rearing practices in families of 60 fifth graders divided into high and low verbal ability groups on the PMA.

In the Kauai study we found for both sexes higher correlations between the children's IQs at age 10 and the educational stimulation in the home than between measures of parental ability and children's IQs. This finding is similar to the results of a study by Wolf (1964) of the relationship between the quality of the home and the intelligence of fifth graders in Chicago. He also reported higher correlations between ratings of intellectual stimulation in the home and children's IQs than those usually found between children's IQ and parental IQ, socioeconomic status, or parental education.

In the Kauai sample, girls' IQs correlated higher than those of the boys with all environmental ratings at age 10, especially with the ratings of educational stimulation in the home. This finding is similar to that reported by Crandall et al. (1964) in a study of 40 early-grade-school children at the Fels Institute. Parents' attitudes and behavior toward their children's intellectual achievement efforts were associated more frequently and more significantly with their daughters' performance on scholastic tests than with that of their sons. Crandall hypothesized that the girls' achievement strivings are more related to the desire for approval from adults while boys' achievement behaviors are more autonomously determined. Because of this, parents' attitudes and behavior (such as satisfaction-dissatisfaction with the child's intellectual performance, parental instigation and participation in intellectual activities with the children) might have less impact and be less predictive of the scholastic performance of boys this age than girls.

In conclusion, the findings with the Kauai sample do not support the Bayley-Schaefer hypothesis that the intellectual performance of boys is more responsive to environmental events while that of girls has a larger component of genetic control. Were this the case we would expect higher same-sex correlations between mothers and daughters, and lower correlations between the environmental ratings and girls' IQs than were found in this study.

The findings of our study do, however, agree with those of the Berkeley Guidance Study and the Fels longitudinal study, and point to sex differences in rate (size and timing) of intellectual maturation, favoring the girls, and to a greater responsiveness of the girls to achievement demands and educational stimulation in the home in middle childhood.

CHAPTER 12

Summary and Conclusions

THE KAUAI STUDY was unique in that it covered all pregnancies and births which occurred in an entire community—over a wide socioeconomic and ethnic spectrum—for more than a decade. We were able to gain a perspective on the magnitude of reproductive and environmental casualties, on the short- and long-term effects of perinatal stress and a deprived environment, and on the predictive value of pediatric-psychologic examinations in early childhood. We were able to document the milieu and growth pattern of a substantial number of children from homes at the lower end of the socioeconomic scale, and to illustrate early differences in ability and achievement among children from ethnic groups on whom little cross-cultural research has been done so far. In sum, here are the highlights of our findings.

MAGNITUDE OF REPRODUCTIVE AND ENVIRONMENTAL CASUALTIES

1. Of pregnancies reaching four weeks gestation, an estimated 237 per 1,000 ended in loss of the conceptus, with the rate of loss forming a decreasing curve from a high of 108 per 1,000 women under observation in the four–seven-weeks period to a low of three in the period 32–35 weeks of gestation.

2. Neonatal, infant, and childhood mortality rates on Kauai were all very low, reflecting a near-minimum number of unfavorable postnatal influences. The perinatal mortality rate based upon fetal deaths of 20 weeks and more and upon infant deaths under 28 days was 35.9 per 1,000 pregnancies. The number of reported fetal deaths of 20 or more weeks was almost twice the number of deaths during the first month after birth. There were 11.7 first-week deaths per 1,000 live births and 13.8 deaths under 28 days.

130

3. The live-born were classified according to presence and severity of physical and mental handicapping conditions of perinatal origin, and estimates were made of the type of care that would be required. In the first two years of life, minor perinatal handicaps had been recognized in 7 percent of the live-born in the time sample: 6.3 percent had conditions requiring short-term medical and nursing services, largely prematurity care and physical defects requiring surgery and other specialized care; 3.7 percent were severely handicapped and required long-term medical, special educational, or custodial services. This last group included children with severe physical defects, children with combined physical defects and mental retardation (IQ below 70), and a group of mentally retarded children without recognizable physical defects by age two.

4. By age 10, 6.6 percent of the children in the time sample were moderately or severely physically handicapped as a result of physical and/or mental defects. Included were 2.3 percent in classes for the mentally retarded. Ten percent of the children were in grades below their chronological age. Forty percent received grades of D or F in one or several basic skill subjects. In each subject more than one-fourth of all children had grades of D and about 5 percent were failing. About one-fourth had some behavior problems.

5. Among services needed for these children by age 10, by far the greatest demand was for remedial help in the basic skill subjects. Twenty-one percent of the children were in need of long-term help and 18 percent, of short-term help. Over five times as many children required special educational services (39 percent) as those who required special medical care, and almost twice as many had serious emotional problems interfering with school progress (13 percent). The greatest need of these 10-year-olds— required by almost one-third of them—was for long-term educational or mental health services or both.

6. In sum, for each 1,000 live births on Kauai there were an estimated 1,311 pregnancies that had advanced to four weeks gestation, 286 having ended in fetal deaths before 20 weeks gestation and 25 more between 20 weeks and term. The 1,000 live births yielded an estimated 844 surviving children at age two who were free of any observed physical defect requiring special care and who had IQs of at least 85. By age 10, only 660 of these children were functioning adequately in school and had no recognized physical, intellectual, or behavior problem. *Thus, during the span of the months of pregnancy and the first decade*

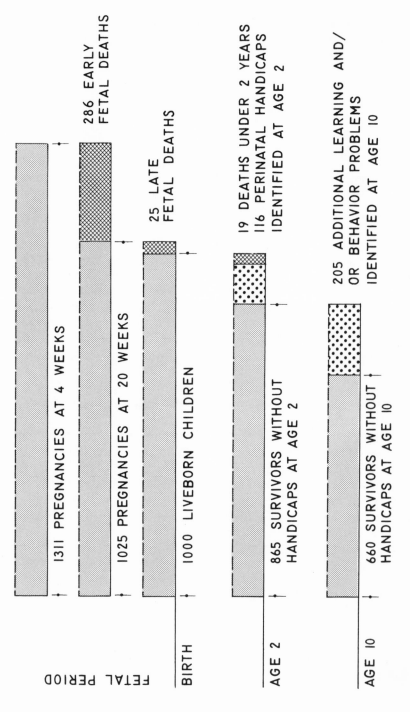

FIGURE 7. Reproductive and environmental casualities in the Kauai study

1311 PREGNANCIES AT 4 WEEKS

286 EARLY FETAL DEATHS

1025 PREGNANCIES AT 20 WEEKS

25 LATE FETAL DEATHS

1000 LIVEBORN CHILDREN

19 DEATHS UNDER 2 YEARS
116 PERINATAL HANDICAPS IDENTIFIED AT AGE 2

865 SURVIVORS WITHOUT HANDICAPS AT AGE 2

205 ADDITIONAL LEARNING AND/ OR BEHAVIOR PROBLEMS IDENTIFIED AT AGE 10

660 SURVIVORS WITHOUT HANDICAPS AT AGE 10

FETAL PERIOD

BIRTH

AGE 2

AGE 10

132

of life, the reproductive and environmental casualties in this community amounted to about one-half of those conceived and about one-third of the live-born (see figure 7).

BIRTH WEIGHT AND GESTATIONAL DIFFERENCES

1. While the overall incidence of low birth weight (2,500 grams or under) was 7.4 percent, it was estimated that 3.2 percent were the small normal babies of small mothers (because of the characteristics of our study population, this proportion is probably higher than it would be in many mainland communities); 2.6 percent were gestationally premature (less than 37 weeks gestation); and 1.6 percent were dysmature.

2. The proportion of infants with birth weight of 2,500 grams or less, both after less than 37 weeks gestation and after 37 weeks or more, was highest for mothers (a) with a history of giving birth to small infants, (b) who gained less than 10 pounds during pregnancy, (c) were of short stature, and (d) were unmarried. A history of previous fetal deaths increased the chance of giving birth to small, preterm infants, and a low prepregnancy weight was associated with small babies born at term (dysmatures). The percentages were highest for mothers in the lowest socioeconomic group for most variables.

3. Except for the very few babies (less than 1 percent) weighing less than 1,500 grams at birth, the much larger group weighing 1,500–2,500 grams had approximately the same proportion of intellectual, emotional, and physical problems as did their peers who had been born heavier; only for perceptual problems did they have a significant excess.

INFLUENCE OF PERINATAL STRESS AND QUALITY OF ENVIRONMENT DURING THE FIRST TWO YEARS

1. With increasing severity of perinatal stress, there was a significant increase in the proportion of children who, by age two, were rated "below normal" in physical development and intellectual status. This retardation was especially pronounced in children with moderate to severe complications. The effects of perinatal stress appeared to be greater among children whose parents were poor, had little education, or were unstable, than among children whose parents were better off economically, better educated, and more stable.

2. Even before they reached their second birthday, children

who had been born to mothers rated low in intelligence or with little education, and/or who were growing up in homes which were providing poorly for their physical and emotional needs, had a substantially higher proportion of "below normal" status ratings than did children growing up in a more favorable family environment. This was true whether or not the children had had perinatal complications.

3. Cattell IQ differences between children with severe perinatal stress growing up in a favorable early environment and those with stress growing up in an unfavorable environment were much larger than differences between children with and without perinatal complications growing up in an adequate family environment.

INFLUENCE OF PERINATAL STRESS AND QUALITY OF ENVIRONMENT DURING THE FIRST 10 YEARS

1. By age 10, differences found between children who had suffered varying degrees of perinatal complications and those who had been born without stress were less pronounced than at age two, and were centered on a small group of survivors of severe perinatal stress. These survivors had a significantly higher proportion of major physical handicaps, predominantly of the central nervous, musculoskeletal, and sensory systems, as well as a higher proportion of IQs below 85 and of placements in special classes or institutions for the mentally retarded. They also had significantly lower mean scores on the verbal comprehension, reasoning, and perceptual and numerical factors on the PMA.

2. Aside from children in institutions, no significant differences were found between children with and without perinatal complications in the proportion of poor grades obtained in basic skill subjects, and in the incidence of language, perceptual, and behavioral problems.

3. Ratings of the families' socioeconomic status, educational stimulation, and emotional support showed significant associations with achievement, intellectual, and emotional problems at age 10. *Ten times more children had problems attributed to the effects of a poor environment than to the effects of serious perinatal stress.*

4. At age 10, differences in mean PMA IQs between children growing up in the most and least favorable home environments were much larger than those between children from the most and least severely stressed groups. The effects of environmental deprivation were more powerful than was apparent at age two, and

accounted for much more of the variance in IQ than degree of perinatal stress.

PREDICTIVE VALUE OF EARLY PEDIATRIC AND PSYCHOLOGIC EXAMINATIONS

1. The diagnoses for children with significant handicaps— physical, mental, or both—by age two were largely confirmed at age 10.

2. The poorest rate of prediction among the physical health problems involved children with eye defects. Only half of those children identified as having strabismus at age two had had any eye problem diagnosed by age 10. An equal number of additional eye problems had been diagnosed by that time, some severe enough to affect school progress. Some might have been prevented by earlier diagnosis with special sensory screening procedures.

3. The best single predictor of IQ and achievement at age 10 was the Cattell IQ score at age two. A combination of Cattell IQ, pediatricians' rating, SQ, perinatal stress score, and parental SES yielded a moderately high positive correlation (R .58) with 10-year IQ, with most of the added predictive power contributed by parental SES. For children with IQs below 80 at age two, a combination of Cattell IQ and pediatricians' ratings of intelligence yielded a high positive correlation (R .80) with the IQ score at 10 years.

4. A combination of deprived environment and retarded intellectual development noted by pediatricians and/or psychologists for children before age two more accurately predicted later serious school-achievement problems than did either the examinations or environmental ratings alone.

ETHNIC DIFFERENCES

1. Infant mortality rates have dropped sharply among the two largest immigrant groups to Kauai, the Japanese and the Filipinos; the Hawaiian population has shown a lower rate of improvement.

2. When social class was held constant, significant differences in achievement and ability remained among children from the five ethnic groups on Kauai, at 2 and 10 years. Significant differences were also found in the language styles and the amount of educational stimulation transmitted by their families. Children of Filipino, Hawaiian, and Portuguese descent had lower mean scores

on the Cattell and PMA tests, and more achievement and behavioral problems than did Anglo-Caucasian and Japanese children.

SEX DIFFERENCES

1. A difference between the sexes in the rate of intellectual maturation favored the girls from ages 2 to 10 years, resulting in higher correlations between their IQs and measures of parental ability than for the boys.

2. Girls appeared to be more responsive than boys to achievement demands made by the family. The difference between the sexes in favor of the girls was significant for all environmental ratings, especially educational stimulation.

IMPLICATIONS

The findings of the Kauai Pregnancy and Child Study contribute to a better understanding of the quantitative and qualitative aspects of reproductive casualties and the crucial role played by the early environment in influencing child development.

When Knobloch and Pasamanick first introduced the concept of a "continuum of reproductive casualties" (1959; 1960), it was recognized that perinatal and infant mortality is only one aspect of reproductive wastage. A decade later, Quilligan (1968) wrote:

> The submerged proportion of the iceberg which can sink families or even societies, is those individuals, who do not die at birth, but who through damage during pregnancy, labor, and delivery, or the neonatal period, are never able to achieve their full potential as productive citizens. We have absolutely no idea of the magnitude of the problem. We have several ways of looking at the intrauterine fetus, starting from early pregnancy, to predict the fetal outcome of life and death. But there have been almost no studies of infants who live to see how they performed in the sixth grade in school.

The results of the Kauai study help to fill some of the gaps in our knowledge. We now have more realistic estimates of the proportion of fetal deaths at various stages of gestation; of the nature and extent of handicapping conditions resulting from damage incurred by the fetus during intrauterine life and during birth; the development and progress in school of the handicapped children in relation to that of their peers without such handicaps;

the influence of the environment on the development in the crucial early years of life; and the impact of the community of the children affected by both perinatal stress and a poor environment during the first decade of life.

Our study was conducted in a community with medical, public health, educational, and mental health services that compare favorably with most communities of similar size on the United States mainland. In spite of this, the magnitude of the "casualties"—reproductive and environmental—among the young in the first decade of life was impressive.

It appears that deleterious biological effects resulting in reproductive casualties exert their peak influence in the very early weeks of pregnancy, when 90 percent of the fetal losses occur. As pregnancy advances and during labor, delivery, and early life, the external environment exerts an increasing influence. The effects of a stimulating or deprived environment appear to be most powerful in the early years of childhood when the greatest degree of rapid growth and development takes place.

Although those who are biologically more vulnerable appear also to be more vulnerable to the stress of a poor environment, it must be remembered that they represent only a very small proportion of all the children who, at the end of the first decade of their lives, fail to function adequately.

Our data suggest that ten times more children in this community had problems attributable to the effects of a poor early environment than to the effects of serious perinatal stress.

THE NEED FOR SETTING PRIORITIES

There is an urgent need to reevaluate present efforts to deal with the enormous load of school achievement and mental health problems encountered among the young in most communities. Available professional skills, time, and resources need to be reallocated according to the magnitude of the needs and the critical time periods at which intervention will be most effective.

The relatively generous support of health services for physically handicapped children and the seriously mentally retarded must be more than matched by an allocation of resources and skills directed to prevention at the earliest stages of learning and to remedial educational and mental health services for a much larger proportion of the communities' children.

CRITICAL PERIODS FOR PREVENTION
AND INTERVENTION

The results of our study and those of longitudinal investigations of the last decade suggest that the critical time for intervention—that time which offers the greatest promise of substantially reducing the number of "casualties" among the young—should come early in childhood, *before* damage is done, rather than depending upon remedial measures later, as is the present practice.

Need for closer cooperation between the various professions attending the birth and care of the child is indicated in order to spot early developmental failures in children suffering from deleterious perinatal conditions and to provide them with a supportive and stimulating environment to minimize the effects of early damage.

Hospital, birth, and physicians' records contain information about the newborn indicating potential trouble—information that is seldom available to community agencies for utilization in planning with the family for the special needs of high-risk infants.

The results of our two-year examinations suggest that every young child in the community should have at least one good medical and developmental examination in early childhood. Careful hearing and vision screening should be included, as well as an appraisal of physical and mental development. Such examinations would provide the focus for early corrective health measures and prevention of crippling behavior and learning problems.

Our analysis of the relationship between the developmental status of the two-year-old children and the quality of their early family environment leaves little doubt that—aside from poor birth histories—parental language styles, attitudes toward achievement, and involvement and concern with the young child have a significant impact on his development *before* he reaches his second birthday.

Preliminary findings of current preschool programs for the disadvantaged (Weickart 1967) suggest that the experiences offered by the environment to the disadvantaged child are inadequate for continued normal intellectual development after age one, and that projects which deal with the enrichment of the environment of the children at ages three, four, or five are remedial rather than preventive. Inasmuch as the damaging effects of a poor postnatal environment are already apparent in the second year of life, it appears necessary to provide enrichment programs much earlier than is currently the practice. Much work needs to be done to evaluate the effectiveness of preventive projects in this period of life.

The establishment of day-care centers for infants and young children would make it possible for all agencies that serve children to pool their resources to provide more efficient physical and mental health services as well as to provide cultural and educational stimulation for the children and their parents. This might be one effective way to stem the tide of problems which are overwhelming the schools.

In reviewing the school records of the ten-year-olds, we were impressed by the great amount of useful information that had been accumulated about these children through routine group testing. School failures could have been successfully spotted in the first three grades if better use had been made of the information already available on the children. More than half of the school failures detected at age 10 in our study could have profited substantially from short-term remedial work in the first three grades by teachers' aides and by volunteer tutors at the critical period when the motivation to achieve and future level of achievement are stabilized.

THE NEED FOR MULTIDISCIPLINARY SERVICE, TRAINING, AND RESEARCH

The Kauai study, from its inception, utilized the insights, methods, and skills of several professions concerned with maternal and child health and development, and involved a number of institutions and community agencies. An effective community program for children also requires a multidisciplinary approach and the successful cooperation of concerned agencies.

A workable example of multidisciplinary cooperation was the study-staff review panel, consisting of a pediatrician, a psychologist, and a public health nurse, who jointly reviewed the combined screening and diagnostic examinations, prepared a final assessment of each child's physical, intellectual, and emotional status, an estimate of the effect of any existing handicap on school progress, and a recommendation for various types of care. The panel sent reports to parents, physicians, schools, and other caretaking agencies in order to initiate remedial measures or therapy.

The services of panels of this type, augmented by other disciplines as indicated, would greatly facilitate diagnostic and follow-up services for young children and those of school age and should be within the reach of every child and family. In-service training of students in the child-care professions by participation in such panels would not only alleviate pressing manpower needs, but would create a greater awareness of the need to break down professional barriers that hinder effective communication and effective action.

In recent years, behavioral scientists have gained much knowledge from multidisciplinary studies that explored the effects of biological stress on behavior and development. There may well be a need now to reciprocate this learning experience by making the health and medical professions familiar with the accumulating store of knowledge from longitudinal studies of child development, studies of the effects of the social environment on development, and the research methods that have proven to be the most valid and reliable in the evaluation of the intervention programs.

ASSESSMENT OF THE ENVIRONMENT AND ENVIRONMENTAL CHANGE

An area in which both biologically and behaviorally oriented students of child growth and development could benefit from joint research is the further exploration of the key factors in the environment that have a cumulative, long-term effect upon the development of children and upon the limits of change that can be brought about by environmental manipulation, especially in the early years of life.

We found it reassuring, for instance, that IQ changes from two to 10 years in our predominantly Oriental and Polynesian populations were very similar to those hypothesized by Bloom (1964, p. 72) as the probable effects of stimulating versus deprived environments on the development of intelligence. Bloom's speculations were based on longitudinal studies of predominantly middle-class Caucasian children.

We found the family interview a helpful tool in the assessment of those qualities of the home which have a significant effect on the child's cognitive and affective development. The educational-stimulation rating differentiated better between good and poor outcomes at age 10 than did the cruder measures of the home environment generally in use, i.e., socioeconomic status, parents' education, and parents' occupation. It also predicted the children's IQ at 10 years better than did measures of parental intelligence.

Such an assessment of the environment might become a useful instrument for early recognition of families who, because of poverty, lack of education, or lack of interest in learning, might not be able to provide the educational stimulation, emotional support, health care, and material advantages necessary to insure the normal development of their children. It could also be useful for selecting children who lack the proper language models, reinforcement, experience, and facilities in the home, and also for evaluating the extent of environmental change that could be brought about by programs of prevention and intervention. This study has made it abundantly clear that the "environmental casualties" among our children need our help as urgently and as early as the "reproductive casualties."

Summary of Scoring System for Prenatal-Perinatal Complications

Mild (Score 1)	Moderate (Score 2)	Severe (Score 3)
mild: pre-eclampsia, essential hypertension, renal insufficiency or anemia; controlled diabetes or hypothyroidism; positive Wasserman and no treatment; acute genitourinary infection third trimester; untreated pelvic tumor producing dystocia; treated asthma	marked: pre-eclampsia, essential hypertension, renal insufficiency or anemia; diabetes under poor control; decompensated cardiovascular disease requiring treatment; untreated thyroid dysfunction; confirmed rubella first trimester; nonobstetrical surgery: general anesthesia, abdominal incision or hypotension	eclampsia; renal or diabetic coma; treated pelvic tumor
vaginal bleeding second or third trimester; placental infarct; marginal placenta previa; premature rupture of membranes; amnionitis; abnormal fetal heart rate; meconium–stained amniotic fluid (exclude if breech); confirmed polyhydramnios	vaginal bleeding with cramping; central placenta previa; partial placenta abruptio; placental or cord anomalies	complete placenta abruptio; congenital syphilis of the newborn
rapid, forceful, or prolonged unproductive labor; frank breech or persistent occiput posterior; twins; elective cesarean section; low forceps with complica-	chin, face, brow, or footling presentation; emergency cesarean section; manual or forceps rotation, midforceps, high forceps or breech and oxygen ad-	transverse lie; emergency cesarean section; manual rotation, midforceps, high forceps or breech extraction and oxygen administered five minutes or more

Mild (Score 1)	Moderate (Score 2)	Severe (Score 3)
tions; cord prolapsed or twisted and oxygen administered to newborn	ministered under five minutes	
breathing delayed one–three minutes; intermittent central cyanosis and oxygen administered under one minute; cry weak or abnormal; bradycardia	breathing delayed three–five minutes; gasping; intermittent central cyanosis and oxygen administered over one minute; cry delayed 5–15 minutes	breathing delayed over five minutes; no respiratory effort; persistent cyanosis and oxygen administered continuously; cry delayed over 15 minutes
birth injury exclusive of central nervous system; jaundice; hemorrhagic disease mild; pneumonia, rate of respiration under 40 and oxygen administered intermittently; birth weight 1,800–2,500 grams and oxygen administered intermittently or incubator or other special care; oral antibiotic to newborn; abnormal tone or Moro reflex; irritability	major birth injury and temporary central-nervous-system involvement; spasms; pneumonia, rate of respiration over 40 and oxygen administered intermittently; apnea and oxygen administered intermittently or resuscitation under five minutes; 1,800–2,500 grams, fair suck and oxygen administered intermittently or incubator; antibiotics administered intravenously; cry absent	major birth injury and persistent central-nervous-system involvement; exchange transfusion; seizure; hyaline membrane disease; pneumonia, rate of respiration over 60 and oxygen administered continuously, resuscitation over five minutes; under 1,800 grams oxygen administered or special feeding; meningitis; absent Moro reflex

Teacher's Checklist

TEACHER'S CHECKLIST

Grade _____   School _____

1. THE CHILD STUDY IS INTERESTED IN IDENTIFYING THOSE CHILDREN WHO, IN THE JUDGMENT OF
    THEIR TEACHER, ARE PERFORMING BELOW THE AVERAGE FOR THEIR GRADE LEVEL.
    IN YOUR JUDGMENT, WHAT IS THIS CHILD'S ACTUAL PERFORMANCE IN THE FOLLOWING SUBJECTS?

Subject	GRADE				
	A Superior	B Above Average	C Average	D Below Average	E Failing
Reading					
Mathematics					
Writing (grammar spelling)					

DO YOU THINK THIS CHILD COULD DO BETTER   No   Yes   (circle)

IF YOU CIRCLED "YES" (THAT HE COULD DO BETTER), ON WHAT DO YOU BASE THIS ANSWER?

Circle appropriate answer

2. DOES HE MAKE GOOD USE OF HIS TIME?   S*   NTI*

3. DOES HE LISTEN CAREFULLY?   S   NTI

4. DOES HE FOLLOW DIRECTIONS?   S   NTI

*S—Satisfactory   *NTI—Needs to improve

146

5. DOES THIS CHILD TEND TO SPEAK: Standard English   or   Island dialect (pidgin)
(Circle correct answer)

6. HAVE YOU NOTICED ANYTHING UNUSUAL ABOUT HIS SPEECH, SUCH AS

a. Groping for the right word?	No	Yes*	* If you circled "yes"
b. Substituting gestures for words?	No	Yes*	( ) please describe and/or
c. Persistent confusion of words	No	Yes*	( ) give examples below.
d. Other — explain			( )

Are you concerned about this child in any of the following areas?
Please circle "no" or "yes" for each question. If "yes", please underline
the most appropriate description and explain in the space provided.
(circle one)

(Please give explanation if "yes" circled)

_____

7. No Yes   POOR HAND COORDINATION IN WRITING, DRAWING, OR MANUAL WORK

8. No Yes   MIRROR WRITING, FAULTY ALIGNMENT OF WORDS, REVERSES LETTERS

9. No Yes   APPEARANCE OR ACTION THAT INDICATES CHILD MAY NOT BE WELL

10. No Yes   ABNORMAL GAIT IN RUNNING OR WALKING

11. No Yes   DROPS THINGS FREQUENTLY

12. No Yes   STUTTERING OR STAMMERING

13. No Yes   LISPING OR ARTICULATION DIFFICULTIES

14. No Yes   ANY NERVOUS HABITS? UNDERLINE. TICS, PERSISTENT MANNERISMS, CLEARING THROAT, SNIFFING, HUNCHING UP SHOULDERS, SQUINTING, TWITCHING OF ANY FACIAL MUSCLES, TAPPING WITH FEET, NAILBITING, THUMBSUCKING, OTHER.

15. No Yes   HYPERACTIVE, INABILITY TO SIT STILL IN CLASS

147

16.	No	Yes	UNCONTROLLED EMOTIONS, TEMPER TANTRUMS
17.	No	Yes	MARKED INABILITY TO CONCENTRATE, DISTRACTIBLE
18.	No	Yes	EXTREMELY IRRITABLE
19.	No	Yes	UNUSUAL FEAR OR ANXIETY
20.	No	Yes	VERY UNHAPPY, DEPRESSED
21.	No	Yes	LACK OF SELF-CONFIDENCE, PRONOUNCED SHYNESS
22.	No	Yes	BULLYING, OVER-AGGRESSIVE, CONSTANTLY QUARRELING
23.	No	Yes	NEGATIVISTIC
24.	No	Yes	FREQUENT LYING
25.	No	Yes	PERSISTENT STEALING
26.	No	Yes	DESTRUCTIVE
27.	No	Yes	TRUANTS FROM SCHOOL

Family Interview

FAMILY INTERVIEW

1. INTERVIEWER   DATE

   (Circle when appropriate)

2. PERSON INTERVIEWED: Father   Mother   Other

3. ALL LIVING CHILDREN BORN IN THIS FAMILY, INCLUDING THOSE AWAY FROM HOME:

a. Child's name (Start with oldest) (Include Study Child)	b. Birthdate	c. Male or Female	d. In school?	e. Grade in regular school or last grade finished*	f. Live in home most of year?
1.		M F	Yes No		Yes No
2.		M F	Yes No		Yes No
3.		M F	Yes No		Yes No
4.		M F	Yes No		Yes No
5.		M F	Yes No		Yes No
6.		M F	Yes No		Yes No
7.		M F	Yes No		Yes No
8.		M F	Yes No		Yes No
9.		M F	Yes No		Yes No
10.		M F	Yes No		Yes No

Over (Circle if additional names on the other side)

*If of High School age, not graduated and not in school, explain

150

4. PARENTS IN HOUSEHOLD: Mother of child: Yes   No   Father of child: Yes   No

5. OTHERS IN HOUSEHOLD: RELATIONSHIP TO CHILD   Adult (over 21)   Child (age)

6. HAVE YOU OR YOUR HUSBAND HAD ANY OPERATION OR ILLNESS THAT MIGHT HAVE PREVENTED YOU FROM HAVING ANY MORE BABIES?

       No   Yes – wife   Yes – husband   If they specify:

7. WOULD YOU BE WILLING TO TELL US WHETHER YOU USE RHYTHM OR ANY OTHER KIND OF BIRTH CONTROL?

       No information   Don't use   Use: If they specify:

8. FATHER'S OCCUPATION: LEVEL

9. FATHER'S EMPLOYER:

10. a. HAS THE FATHER WORKED STEADILY SINCE   WAS BORN?   Yes   No   If no:

    b. WHY NOT?

    c. FOR HOW LONG NOT EMPLOYED?   d. WHEN?

11. a. HAS THE MOTHER WORKED OUTSIDE THE HOME SINCE   WAS BORN?   No   Yes   If yes:

    b. FULL TIME OR PART TIME (circle)

    c. WHEN?

    d. WHO TOOK CARE OF THE CHILD?

12. FATHER'S EDUCATION: (Circle the last grade of regular school completed)

    a. 1   2   3   4   5   6   7   8   9   10   11   12   13   14   15   16   16+   1   2   3
                                                       (vocational or other)

    b. DID HE GO TO HIGH SCHOOL ON KAUAI?   No   Yes   If yes, complete Form 10.

    c. WAS ALL SCHOOLING RECEIVED OUTSIDE U.S.?   No   Yes: Japan   Philippines   Other
                                                            (to be circled)

151

13. MOTHER'S EDUCATION: (Circle the last grade of regular school completed)

a. 1 2 3 4 5 6 7 8 9 10 11 12 13 14 15 16 16+ 1 2 3
                                                    (vocational or other)

b. DID SHE GO TO HIGH SCHOOL ON KAUAI?   No   Yes   If yes, complete Form 10.

c. WAS ALL SCHOOLING RECEIVED OUTSIDE U.S.?   No   Yes: Japan   Philippines   Other
                                                            (to be circled)

14. a. IS ENGLISH THE USUAL LANGUAGE SPOKEN IN YOUR HOME?   Yes   No

b. IS ANOTHER LANGUAGE ALSO SPOKEN?   No   Yes: Japanese   Filipino   Other
                                                    (to be circled)

c. DID _____ LEARN TO UNDERSTAND THIS LANGUAGE?   No   Yes
   SPEAK IT?   No   Yes

d. TO WHAT EXTENT DO YOUR CHILDREN SPEAK PIDGIN AT HOME?   Often   Rarely (is discouraged)

e. TO WHAT EXTENT DO YOU OR YOUR HUSBAND SPEAK PIDGIN AT HOME?   Often   Rarely or never

15. DID SOMEONE OFTEN READ BOOKS TO THIS CHILD BEFORE HE ENTERED SCHOOL?
    No   Yes   WHO?

16. DOES _____ OFTEN READ BOOKS OR MAGAZINES OTHER THAN THOSE REQUIRED BY THE SCHOOL?
    (Exclude comics)   No   Yes

17. WHAT KINDS OF THINGS DO YOU READ?   None   A little   More than a little
    Specify:

(Skip if no spouse)

18. WHAT KINDS OF THINGS DOES YOUR HUSBAND (WIFE) READ: None   A little   More than a little
    Specify:

19. DOES _____ HAVE OUTSIDE INTERESTS, SUCH AS LESSONS, GROUP ACTIVITIES, HOBBIES?
    No   Yes (List)

152

20. a. DOES HE HAVE HOMEWORK?   No   Yes   If yes:

    b. DOES HE USUALLY COMPLETE IT?   No   Yes

    c. WHERE DOES HE DO HIS HOMEWORK; (Describe conditions):

    (Skip if no spouse)

21. DO YOU AND YOUR HUSBAND (WIFE) DISCUSS WITH EACH OTHER ———— 'S SCHOOL WORK?
    No   Yes;   EXPLAIN

22. IS ———— GIVEN RESPONSIBILITY FOR DOING CERTAIN THINGS?
    No   Yes;   WHAT?

23. DOES ———— HAVE SEVERAL FRIENDS HIS OWN AGE?
    Yes   No;   EXPLAIN:

24. ARE THERE ADULTS OUTSIDE THE FAMILY ———— LIKES TO BE WITH?
    No   Yes;   WHO?

25. HAVE ANY OF THE FOLLOWING THINGS HAPPENED TO YOUR FAMILY IN THE LAST 10 YEARS?
    (Exclude Study Child for f and g)

			Date From	To
a. Separation from spouse	No	Yes		
b. Desertion of spouse	No	Yes		
c. Death of spouse	No	Yes		
d. Divorce	No	Yes		
e. Remarriage	No	Yes		
f. Serious illness	No	Yes	Explanations (identify by letter):	

153

g. Hospitalization
    (long or frequent)   No   Yes
h. Serious worries   No   Yes
i. Drinking problem   No   Yes
j. Frequent quarrels   No   Yes
k. Other   No   Yes

26. HAVE YOU USED THE SERVICES OF ANY SOCIAL AGENCY SINCE THIS CHILD WAS BORN?
     No   Yes;   WHICH?   Dates From ___ To ___ Reason

27. DO YOU DO THINGS TOGETHER AS A FAMILY?
     No   Yes;   WHAT?

28. DO YOU AND _____ DO THINGS TOGETHER?   No   Yes;   examples:

(Skip if no spouse)

29. DOES YOUR HUSBAND (WIFE) AND _____ DO THINGS TOGETHER?
     No   Yes;   examples:

30. DOES _____ TALK ABOUT HIS ACTIVITIES OR PROBLEMS WITH YOU?
     No   Yes;   examples:

(Skip if no spouse)

31. DOES _____ TALK ABOUT HIS ACTIVITIES OR PROBLEMS WITH HIS FATHER (MOTHER)?
     No   Yes;   examples:

154

32. WHAT ARE SOME OF THE THINGS _____ DOES THAT PLEASE YOU?
    Nothing   Specify:

33. a. HOW DO YOU LET HIM (HER) KNOW THAT YOU ARE PLEASED?

    (Skip if no spouse)
    b. HOW DOES THE FATHER (MOTHER) LET HIM (HER) KNOW WHEN HE IS PLEASED?

34. IS THIS CHILD EASY TO MANAGE?   Yes   No;   EXPLAIN:

    (Skip if no spouse)
35. DO YOU AND YOUR HUSBAND (WIFE) HAVE DIFFICULTY IN AGREEING ON HOW TO MANAGE THIS
    CHILD?
    No   Yes;   EXPLAIN: Yes   No

36. a. DOES _____ USUALLY DO WHAT YOU TELL HIM TO DO?
    b. IF HE DOES NOT, HOW DO YOU TRY TO MAKE HIM MIND?
    (Parent's own words)

Interviewer's Impressions
    Check one or more

☐ Explain sometimes
☐ Rarely or never explain
☐ Repeat, scold, yell
☐ Withhold privileges
☐ Physical force

155

37. HAS _____ HAD ANY SERIOUS CONDITIONS, ILLNESSES OR ACCIDENTS REQUIRING VISIT TO A DOCTOR?   No   Yes;   describe:

(What was wrong?)   (When was child ill?)   (Name of doctor)

38. HAS _____ BEEN HOSPITALIZED?   No   Yes;   describe:

(Name of hospital)   (Date)   (Reason)

39. HAS _____ EVER HAD ANY CONVULSIONS OR SPELLS?   No   Yes   AGE AND DR. SEEN

40. a. HAS _____ HAD ASTHMA SINCE HE (OR SHE) WAS TWO YEARS OLD?   No   Yes   If yes:
     b. WHEN?
     c. HOW OFTEN?
     d. HAS THE DOCTOR GIVEN ANY MEDICINE TO HELP THE CHILD BREATHE BETTER IN AN ASTHMA ATTACK?   No   Yes;   e.   NAME OF DOCTOR

41. DOES _____ SEEM TO TIRE MORE EASILY THAN OTHER CHILDREN?   No   Yes;   EXPLAIN:

156

42. DOES HE (OR SHE) SEEM MORE CLUMSY IN MOVING OR MORE AWKWARD WITH HIS HANDS THAN OTHER CHILDREN?   No   Yes;   EXPLAIN:

43. WHAT HAND DOES THIS CHILD USE TO EAT WITH?   Left   Right   Ambidextrous?

44. WHAT HAND DOES THIS CHILD USE TO WRITE WITH?   Left   Right   Ambidextrous?

45. HAS _____ HAD ANY OF THE FOLLOWING PROBLEMS?

(Past)		(Present)		(Comments)
a. No Yes	Stuttering or stammering.	No	Yes	
b. No Yes	Lisping or trouble in pronouncing words.	No	Yes	
c. No Yes	Does he have any of the following habits: Underline. Tics, persistent mannerisms, clearing throat, sniffing, hunching up shoulders, squinting, twitching of any facial muscles, tapping with feet or hands, nailbiting, thumbsucking; Finicky about eating; bed wetting.			
d. No Yes	Inability to ever sit still.	No	Yes	
e. No Yes	Temper tantrums, uncontrolled emotions.	No	Yes	
f. No Yes	Unable to concentrate, distractible.	No	Yes	
g. No Yes	Extremely irritable.	No	Yes	
h. No Yes	Has unusual fear or anxiety.	No	Yes	
i. No Yes	Very unhappy, depressed much of the time.	No	Yes	
j. No Yes	Lacks self-confidence, extremely shy; feelings hurt easily.	No	Yes	
k. No Yes	Constantly quarreling, over-aggressive.	No	Yes	
l. No Yes	Overly contrary and stubborn.	No	Yes	
m. No Yes	Frequent lying.	No	Yes	
n. No Yes	Persistent stealing.	No	Yes	
o. No Yes	Running away from home or school.	No	Yes	
p. No Yes	Destroying things on purpose.	No	Yes	

46. IS THERE ANYTHING ELSE THAT CONCERNS YOU OR WOULD HELP US TO UNDERSTAND THIS CHILD?

157

47. INFORMATION IS NEEDED FROM THE FOLLOWING:

			Consent Form Obtained	
Physician	Yes	No	Yes	No
Hospital	Yes	No	Yes	No
Dept. of Social Services	Yes	No	Yes	No
Mental Health Service	Yes	No	Yes	No
Other	Yes	No	Yes	No

48. HOUSE (Circle)

Poor	Average	Good
(Crowded, bare necessities)	(Adequate room and equipment)	(Plenty of room, well equipped)

COMMENTS:

158

Case Summaries of Children with High-Low Perinatal Stress and High-Low Educational Stimulation and Emotional Support

Two- and 10-Year Status of Children without Perinatal Complications Who Grew Up in Homes Rated High in Educational Stimulation and Emotional Support

Code No.	Family Characteristics	Two-Year Status	10-Year Status
0175-2 Male	Father business manager, two years college education; mother high school graduate, two years secretarial school; mother rated "intelligent, skillful, good-humored, stable, responsible, outgoing, self-confident, affectionate, happy, permissive, kind, temperate, mature, takes matters in stride"	Physical development normal Cattell IQ 108 Vineland SQ 142 "Agreeable, independent, intelligent, responsive"	PMA IQ 128 Obese No school problems
0244-1 Female	Father executive, college graduate; mother high school graduate, rated "intelligent, resourceful, good-humored, indulgent, kind, temperate, concerned, contented"	Physical development normal Cattell IQ 95 Vineland SQ 90 "Calm, persevering, solemn, uncommunicative"	PMA IQ 123 No school problems
0590-1 Female	Father professional worker, graduate education; mother high school graduate, rated "intelligent, good-humored, stable, responsible, takes matters in stride, relaxed, affectionate, happy, considerate, calm, patient, objective, matter-of-fact"	Physical development normal Cattell IQ 120 "Bright, independent child"	PMA IQ 123 Allergy No school problems
0985-1 Female	Father professional man; mother college graduate, teacher; mother rated "responsible, energetic, warmhearted, affectionate, kind, temperate, takes matters in stride"	Physical development normal Stanford-Binet IQ 137 Vineland SQ 95	PMA IQ 122 No school problems

2074-1 Male	Father professional man, self-employed; both parents college graduates; mother social worker, works part-time as professional assistant, rated "intelligent, skillful, good-humored, stable, responsible, takes matters in stride, relaxed, self-confident, warm-hearted, affectionate, happy, permissive, patient, kind, temperate, contented"	Physical development normal Cattell IQ 100 Vineland SQ 106 "Calm, eager, friendly, independent, relaxed, persevering"	PMA IQ 121 No school problems
1548-1 Female	Father administrator, five years college; mother one year college, rated "intelligent, resourceful, responsible, energetic, warmhearted, considerate, affectionate, kind, temperate, interested, contented, takes matters in stride"	Physical development normal Cattell IQ 105 Vineland SQ 111 "Calm, independent, hesitant, quiet, persevering, serious"	PMA IQ 120 Farsighted in left eye No school problems
0439-1 Male	Father supervising engineer; both parents college graduates; mother teaches full-time since child in nursery school, rated "intelligent, good-humored, stable, responsible, relaxed, self-confident, warmhearted, affectionate, happy, patient, kind, temperate, contented"	Physical development normal Cattell IQ 95 Vineland SQ 114 "Agreeable, solemn"	PMA IQ 119 No school problems
2181-1 Female	Father personnel director; mother teacher; both parents college graduates; mother rated "intelligent, resourceful, good-humored, stable, responsible, energetic, outgoing, relaxed, warmhearted, affectionate, self-controlled, calm, patient, kind, temperate, mature, contented, easygoing"	Physical development superior Cattell IQ 89 Vineland SQ 110 "Bashful, deliberate, determined, quiet"	PMA IQ 117 Nontoxic goiter No school problems

Code No.	Family Characteristics	Two-Year Status	10-Year Status
1107-1 Female	Father professional man, college graduate; mother one year college and supervisory training, rated "good-humored, responsible, takes matters in stride, outgoing, affectionate, happy, considerate, patient, kind, temperate, mature, somewhat overprotective"	Physical development superior Cattell IQ 105 Vineland SQ 100 "Agreeable, cheerful, alert, friendly, responsive"	PMA IQ 117 No school problems
0817-1 Male	Father self-employed businessman, high school graduate and two years vocational training; mother college graduate, employed part-time in father's shop; mother rated "stable, responsible, takes matters in stride, reasonably relaxed, affectionate, happy, calm, kind, temperate, mature, contented"	Physical development normal Cattell IQ 114 Vineland SQ 119	PMA IQ 116 Asthma No school problems
0412-1 Male	Father assistant manager, graduate education; mother college educated, part-time teacher, rated "intelligent, affectionate, happy, patient, concerned"	Physical development superior Cattell IQ 105 Vineland SQ 112 "Active, cheerful, determined, eager, alert, quick, independent, resourceful, responsive"	PMA IQ 116 Unable to sit still; shy, nervous, tense No school problems
1459-1 Female	Father engineer, college graduate; mother eighth-grade education, rated "good-humored, outgoing, affectionate, indulgent, patient, kind, temperate, contented, takes matters in stride"	Physical development normal Cattell IQ 100 Vineland SQ 131 "Anxious, dependent, hesitant"	PMA IQ 116 No school problems

ID / Sex	Family background	Development	PMA
1848-2 Female	Father professional man, self-employed; mother teacher; both parents college graduates; mother rated "intelligent, stable, energetic, considerate, self-controlled, kind, temperate, mature"	Physical development normal. Cattell IQ 122. Vineland SQ 117. "Active, aggressive, independent"	PMA IQ 114. No school problems
0463-1 Male	Both parents teachers and college graduates; mother has worked full-time since child was nine months old; child cared for by grandmother who is rated "good-humored, stable, relaxed, self-confident, warmhearted, affectionate, considerate, easygoing, indulgent, calm, patient"	Physical development normal. Cattell IQ 94. Vineland SQ 117. "Bashful, calm, independent, hesitant, solemn"	PMA IQ 114. Nasal allergy. No school problems
0566-1 Female	Father manager; both parents college graduates; mother teacher, rated "intelligent, skillful, good-humored, relaxed, permissive, affectionate, mature, contented"	Physical development superior. Cattell IQ 106. Vineland SQ 128. "Active, cheerful, eager, energetic, friendly, independent, resourceful, responsive, restless, persevering, quick, sociable"	PMA IQ 111. No school problems
0648-2 Male	Father businessman; parents one year college education; mother rated "intelligent, stable, responsible, takes matters in stride, relaxed, permissive, self-confident, warmhearted, permissive, self-controlled, calm, kind, temperate, mature, contented, indulgent"	Physical development superior. Cattell IQ 94. Vineland SQ 124. "Active, determined, energetic, restless, distractible"	PMA IQ 110. No school problems

Code No.	Family Characteristics	Two-Year Status	10-Year Status
1748-1 Male	Father professional man, college graduate; mother high school graduate, rated "intelligent, resourceful, good-humored, stable, responsible, energetic, takes matters in stride, outgoing, relaxed, affectionate, happy, kind, temperate, mature, contented"	Physical development low normal Cattell IQ 100 Vineland SQ 124 "Alert, resourceful, responsive, persevering"	PMA IQ 110 No school problems
1272-2 Male	Father owns own business; both parents high school graduates; mother one year design school, rated "responsible, energetic, takes matters in stride, relaxed, affectionate, happy, permissive, kind, temperate, contented, somewhat indulgent"	Physical development normal Cattell IQ 95 Vineland SQ 157 "Deliberate, eager, resourceful, persevering, stubborn"	PMA IQ 107 No school problems
0354-1 Female	Father business administrator, college graduate; mother three years of college, rated "intelligent, stable, outgoing, relaxed, self-confident, happy, kind, temperate, matter-of-fact, easygoing, indulgent"	Physical development normal Cattell IQ 88 Vineland SQ 112 "Active, friendly, restless, sociable, talkative, temperamental"	PMA IQ 101 No school problems
0248-2 Female	Father manager, two years of college; mother college graduate, rated "intelligent, good-humored, stable, responsible, relaxed, self-confident, happy, permissive, calm, patient, kind, temperate, matter-of-fact, contented, mature, restrictive"	Physical development normal Cattell IQ 94 Vineland SQ 106 "Agreeable, eager, friendly, relaxed, responsive, sociable"	PMA IQ 101 Asthma No school problems

Two- and 10-Year Status of Children with Severe Perinatal Complications Who Grew Up in Homes Rated High in Educational Stimulation and Emotional Support

Code No.	Perinatal Conditions	Family Characteristics	Two-Year Status	10-Year Status
2133-1 Male	Severe anoxia; 15 minutes to first breath; mouth-to-mouth and oxygen resuscitation; cyanotic when feeding; lethargic; cried only when stimulated; slight jaundice	Father mill supervisor; both parents college-educated; mother rated "active, cooperative, pleasant, handles baby with confidence"	Did not participate in two-year follow-up; family moved to another island	WISC Full IQ 122 Verbal IQ 125 Performance IQ 114 Bender-Gestalt errors 9 Slight perceptual problem in school "Very active"
1967-1 Female	35 hours labor without progress; right occipital transverse position; attempted rotation; cesarean section, blood transfusion, slightly jaundiced infant	Father craftsman; both parents high school graduates; mother rated "relaxed, affectionate, self-controlled, slightly overprotective"	Physical development normal Cattell IQ 95 Vineland SQ 105 "Somewhat hesitant, inclined to turn to mother for help"	PMA IQ 122 Somewhat withdrawn and shy, lacks self-confidence No school problems
0026-1 Male	Severe hypertensive disease throughout pregnancy; cesarean delivery; newborn anoxic, resuscitation by mouth for more than seven minutes; poor color in incubator; jaundiced five days	Father skilled operative worker, eighth grade education; mother tenth-grade education, rated "resourceful, good-humored, stable, takes matters in stride, outgoing, relaxed, affectionate, considerate, patient, kind, temperate, concerned, contented"	Physical development normal; slight clumsiness due to obesity Cattell IQ 105 Advanced verbally "Active, agreeable, cheerful, impulsive, responsive"	PMA IQ 117 Obesity hinders him in running No school problems

Code No.	Perinatal Conditions	Family Characteristics	Two-Year Status	10-Year Status
1782-2 Female	Premature rupture of membrane five days; two hours labor; gestational age 33 weeks; weight 3 pounds 4 ounces; in incubator for one month	Father businessman; parents high school graduates; mother rated "intelligent, resourceful, responsible, energetic, outgoing, self-confident, affectionate, happy, patient, kind, temperate, contented, stimulating, somewhat overprotective and restrictive"	Physical development normal Cattell IQ 104 Vineland SQ 123 "Pleasant, agreeable"	PMA IQ 111 No school problems
0709-1 Female	Mother's diabetes not under good control; hypertension throughout pregnancy; cesarean section	Father businessman; both parents high school graduates; mother rated "stable, takes matters in stride, affectionate, sensibly permissive"; father rated "kind, temperate, mature"	Physical development low normal; questionable energy level Cattell IQ 86 Vineland SQ 82 "Inhibited, passive, solemn, somewhat dependent"	PMA IQ 110 No school problems
0482-1 Male	Pre-eclampsia, meconium-stained amniotic fluid; dystocia; midforceps rotation; newborn cyanotic, resuscitation; in incubator for 15 hours; poor muscle tone	Father craftsman; both parents high school graduates; mother rated "intelligent, skillful, resourceful, good-humored, stable, energetic, responsible, outgoing, self-confident, re-	Physical development normal Mental development normal	PMA IQ 110 Asthma No school problems

	Birth history	Parent description	Physical development	Outcome
		...laxed, affectionate, considerate, permissive, high in maternal capacity,"		
0951-1 Male	Pre-eclampsia; hospitalized in second and third trimester for bleeding; breech extraction; respiration delayed two minutes; resuscitation for 5–10 minutes; pallor	Father clerical worker, high school graduate; mother ninth grade, affectionate, rated "kind, affectionate, temperate, good at handling child"	Physical development normal. Cattell IQ 95. Vineland SQ 105. "Hesitant, slow to cooperate"	PMA IQ 109. Somewhat anxious, nervous, distractible. No school problems
0098-2 Male	Placenta abruptio; cesarean section after 13 hours labor and hemorrhage; newborn two minutes resuscitation; gestational age 34 weeks; weight 4 pounds 12½ ounces	Father supervisor, eleventh-grade education; mother high school graduate, rated "outgoing affectionate, happy, easygoing, kind, temperate"	Physical development a little slow. Cattell IQ 93. Vineland SQ 113. "Active, restless, sociable, healthy, but immature"	PMA IQ 106. No school problems
1254-2 Male	Four hours labor; gestational age 31 weeks; weight 3 pounds 2 ounces, very cyanotic; apnea; oxygen administered; in incubator for 1½ months; poor feeder	Father office worker; both parents high school graduates; mother rated "intelligent, good-humored, stable, responsible, takes matters in stride, affectionate, calm, kind, temperate, matter-of-fact"	Physical development: internal strabismus of right eye. Cattell IQ 78. Vineland SQ 89. "Eye-hand coordination weak, though not grossly impaired; responsive"	PMA IQ 105. Nystagmus; blind right eye. No school problems

Code No.	Perinatal Conditions	Family Characteristics	Two-Year Status	10-Year Status
1174-1 Female	68 hours labor; brow presentation; forceps delivery; delayed breathing; oxygen by catheter; bruised face; marked edema; in incubator; "question of brain damage"	Father farm foreman, ninth-grade education; mother high school graduate, rated "good-humored, stable, responsible, outgoing, self-confident, warm-hearted, affectionate, happy"	Physical development normal Mental development normal	PMA IQ 100 Ds in reading and arithmetic
0795-1 Female	Four-hour delivery; anoxic; respiration delayed for six minutes; resuscitation; remained in hospital because of "immaturity"; gestational age 40 weeks; weight 4 pounds 13 ounces	Father skilled mechanic; both parents high school graduates; mother rated "takes matters in stride, relaxed, permissive, kind, temperate, contented, easygoing"	Physical development normal Cattell IQ 94 Vineland SQ 131 "Calm, inhibited, passive, quiet"	PMA IQ 97 No school problems
1151-1 Female	Cervical neoplasm causing difficult delivery, 28 hours labor; breech; manual extraction; newborn resuscitated; gestational age 37 weeks; weight 4 pounds 8½ ounces; in incubator for 1½ weeks	Father clerical worker; both parents high school graduates; mother rated "intelligent, stable, good-humored, responsible, relaxed, affectionate, kind, temperate, concerned, indulgent"	Physical development retarded; very small with small head Cattell IQ 95 Vineland SQ 130 Low frustration level	PMA IQ 96 D in reading
0766-1 Female	Face presentation; cesarean section after 29	Father skilled operator; both parents high	Physical development normal	WISC Full IQ 96 Verbal IQ 91

Code No.	Family Characteristics	Two-Year Status	10-Year Status
	hours labor; anoxic, resuscitation required; condition fair ... school graduates; mother rated "good-humored, easygoing, affectionate, calm, kind, contented, takes matters in stride"	Cattell IQ 89 Vineland SQ 111 "Anxious, bashful, dependent, fearful, inhibited, tense"	Performance IQ 101 Skeletal abnormalities: ulnar deviation of fingers and metatarsus varus Repeated first grade; D in arithmetic; depressed, lonely, "looks and acts like ugly duckling"
1229-2 Male	Mother mild preeclampsia; newborn anoxic, resuscitated for 10 minutes; in incubator; gestational age 30 weeks; weight 4 pounds 10 ounces ... Father skilled operator; eighth-grade education; mother high school graduate, rated "good-humored, warm-hearted"	Physical development normal Mental development normal Ratings made by pediatrician	PMA IQ 92 WISC Full IQ 80 Verbal IQ 81 Performance IQ 82 One grade below CA; Ds in reading, writing, arithmetic; problems in auditory memory and visual-motor integration

Two- and 10-Year Status of Children Without Perinatal Complications Who Grew Up in Homes Rated Low in Educational Stimulation and Emotional Support

Code No.	Family Characteristics	Two-Year Status	10-Year Status
1087-3 Female	Father farm laborer, often unemployed, has no formal education; mother has second-grade education, works in night shift in cannery while older daughters take care of baby; family gets welfare support whenever husband is ill or unemployed; mother rated "easygoing, indifferent"	Physical development normal Cattell IQ 86 Vineland SQ 105	WISC Full IQ 123 Verbal IQ 119 Performance IQ 124 Ds in grammar, spelling and arithmetic; not motivated, insecure, lacks self-confidence

Code No.	Family Characteristics	Two-Year Status	10-Year Status
1085-2 Male	Father farm laborer, has no formal education; mother has fifth-grade education, was diagnosed as mentally retarded, has had several illegitimate children, neglectful of her children; family has welfare assistance; mother rated "easygoing, careless, indifferent, childlike, irresponsible, easily angered, erratic, impatient." Psychologist notes extreme lack of stimulation in child's background and anticipates progressive retardation	Physical development normal Cattell IQ 100 Vineland SQ 113	WISC Full IQ 108 Verbal IQ 125 Performance IQ 87 Ds in all basic skill subjects; perceptual-motor problem; poor fine motor coordination; chronic nervous habits; bullies, overaggressive, acts out problems
1079-3 Male	Father farm laborer with ninth-grade education; mother seventh-grade education; domestic and financial problems; father left family after birth of 10th child; family on welfare	Physical development normal Cattell IQ 90 Vineland SQ 110	WISC Full IQ 106 Verbal IQ 94 Performance IQ 118 Fs in reading, grammar, spelling and arithmetic; stutters, overalert; confused about absent father; ambivalent about "overpowering" mother; has poor self-image
1910-1 Male	Child illegitimate; mother 16 years old, did not marry father of child, but a man whom she divorced four years later, has had three more illegitimate children; child support from ADC program, no support from former husband	Physical development normal Cattell IQ 100 Vineland SQ 110	PMA IQ 106 Ds in reading, writing, and arithmetic

170

0912-2 Female	Multiple-problem family; father unemployed laborer, family on welfare; father third-grade education, mother eighth-grade education; older children have frequent difficulties because of truancy and antisocial behavior; mother rated "dull, easygoing, careless, childlike, irresponsible"	Physical development low normal Mental development low normal Ratings made by pediatrician Cattell IQ 83 Vineland SQ 117 "Child solemn and uncommunicative; receives no appropriate and adequate attention at home"	PMA IQ 102 Ds in reading, grammar, spelling, and arithmetic
0231-3 Female	Father farm laborer, has seventh-grade education; mother ninth-grade education, works during night shift	Physical development normal Cattell IQ 91 Vineland SQ 96	WISC Full IQ 99 Verbal IQ 94 Performance IQ 104 Ds in reading, writing, arithmetic; reading below grade level; persistently withdrawn, shy, lack of self-confidence; poorly motivated
0621-2 Male	Father technician, seventh-grade education; mother high school graduate. Father quits jobs or gets laid off for lack of suitable employment, leaves island to work away from family for long periods of time; financial problems; family supported by welfare when father unemployed	Physical development normal Cattell IQ 90 Vineland SQ 105	WISC Full IQ 98 Verbal IQ 87 Performance IQ 110 Restless in class

Code No.	Family Characteristics	Two-Year Status	10-Year Status
1164-1 Female	Father laborer; mother barmaid, separated; children live with relative; mother does not provide for child; aunt works full time to support her own and her sister's children; father provides money for groceries when he can, but does not live with family	Physical development normal, but nutritional status only fair. Cattell IQ 107	PMA IQ 96. Poor grades in reading, writing, arithmetic; temper tantrums, restless, sensitive, moody; often absent from school; insecure
0615-2 Male	Father laborer with eighth-grade education; mother 10th-grade education, has had mental illness, since then she has been disorganized, haphazard, and especially disturbed during her pregnancies, poor housekeeper and manager; financial problems; family supported by public welfare; rated "indifferent, irresponsible, negativistic, discontented, hostile, distant, careless, childlike"; still functioning subnormally upon discharge from hospital	Physical development normal. Cattell IQ 74. Vineland SQ 91. "Appears to be a product of cultural impoverishment and maternal neglect"	PMA IQ 95. Fs in reading, writing and arithmetic; short attention span; pronounced shyness; very unhappy; slow of speech
1650-1 Male	Father laborer with no formal education; mother 10th-grade education, rated "unintelligent, unemotional, irresponsible, easygoing, careless"	Physical development normal. Cattell IQ 90. Vineland SQ 93. "Extremely shy"	WISC Full IQ 95. Verbal IQ 90. Performance IQ 101. Poor grades in reading, writing, and arithmetic; insecure, passive, dependent
0808-1	Father laborer, ninth-grade education;	Physical status adequate, but	WISC Full IQ 95

ID / Sex	Family background	Physical/mental development	Test results and behavior
Male	mother high school graduate, works full time at cannery except for maternity leaves; baby sister takes care of child; father does not assume responsibility for child; frequent family quarrels	child suffers from lowered vitality and malaise Cattell IQ 100	Verbal IQ 90 Performance IQ 101 Poor grade in reading; withdrawn, shy, lack of self-confidence; distractible, irritable, and restless
1559-2 Male	Mother divorced, works as barmaid; father has third-grade education, is laborer; mother has fourth-grade education, rated "easy-going, careless, lazy, unintelligent, childlike"	Physical development normal Cattell IQ 112 Vineland SQ 124	PMA IQ 92 Temper tantrums; feelings hurt easily; "nobody likes me"; frequently lying
1400-2 Male	Father laborer; both parents seventh-grade education; live in poor, sparsely furnished home; mother rated "unintelligent, careless, erratic, ambivalent," has had psychiatric help, was in training school for delinquents as a girl. Frequent quarrels at home	Physical development below average; appears malnourished Mental development low normal; speech has not developed	PMA IQ 90 Under par, asthmatic Ds in reading, writing, and arithmetic
0487-2 Male	Mother known to department of social welfare for many years; six of her 10 children, including this boy, illegitimate; the older children have been placed in foster homes; has long history of alcoholism; welfare recipient; gives child poor physical care	Physical development low normal Mental development low normal Ratings made by pediatrician	WISC Full IQ 88 Verbal IQ 95 Performance IQ 82 High frequency hearing loss and small bilateral strabismus Repeated kindergarten and first grade; Ds in writing and arithmetic; hyperactive, restless, distractible

Code No.	Family Characteristics	Two-Year Status	10-Year Status
0264-1 Male	Child illegitimate; mother and father both young teenagers; mother married older man not father of child; mother has eighth-grade education; husband has third-grade education, laborer, often unemployed. Mother rated "indifferent, unintelligent, unemotional, withdrawn, dependent, childlike, suggestible, irresponsible, uncommunicative"	Physical development normal Cattell IQ 92 Vineland SQ 104 "Child tense and hyperactive"	WISC Full IQ 88 Verbal IQ 87 Performance IQ 92 Repeated first grade; current grades: D in reading, writing, and arithmetic
1719-1 Female	Mother has had four husbands and divorces, two of her seven children born out of wedlock, married to girl's father in second trimester of pregnancy, divorced him when child six months old; supported by welfare; mother rated "easygoing, careless, indifferent, irresponsible, discontented"	Physical development normal, but small physique Refused to cooperate on test, but judged low normal in mental development Vineland SQ 110	PMA IQ 88 Ds in reading, writing, and arithmetic Distractible, shy, lacks self-confidence
0958-4 Female	Father unskilled laborer with sporadic work record; multiple-problem family supported by welfare; parents married while mother was pregnant with fourth child; father fourth-grade education; mother 11th-grade education, but mental age of nine year old, operated on for brain tumor at age 14, hospitalized several times for psychotic reactions (paranoid) and postpartum psychoses;	Parents refused pediatric and psychological examinations	PMA IQ 88 Congenital heart murmur; hearing loss (left ear) Ds in reading and arithmetic; persistently withdrawn, shy, lacks self-confidence

174

Case	Background	Development	Test Results
	grandmother also diagnosed psychotic; neglect, truancy, and delinquency of older children; family lives with grandparents in poorly furnished, crowded home. Mother rated "indifferent, unintelligent, demanding, punitive"		WISC Full IQ 87 Verbal IQ 84 Performance IQ 94 D in reading
0177-3 Female	Father farm laborer, third-grade education; mother fourth-grade education; economic difficulties; at times support from welfare; family discord; mother rated "somewhat punitive"	Physical development low normal Mental development low normal Ratings made by pediatrician Cattell IQ 100 Vineland SQ 114	
2163-2 Male	Father farmer and fisherman; both parents high school graduates; inconsistent discipline between adult members of household, strained relationship with in-laws; mother left home when child was one year old, then returned to her husband; mother rated "easily hurt, self-sacrificing, worrisome"	Physical development large Cattell IQ 86 Vineland SQ 90	WISC Full IQ 84 Verbal IQ 79 Performance IQ 93 Repeated first grade; Ds in reading and writing; F in arithmetic; perceptual problem; problem in fine motor coordination; unable to sit still in class, to concentrate; constantly quarreling, negativistic, careless, demands much attention from teachers

Code No.	Family Characteristics	Two-Year Status	10-Year Status
0070-2 Female	Father laborer, 10th-grade education; mother eighth-grade education, works full-time in night shifts as waitress and in cannery while father takes care of eight children; family gets welfare assistance	Physical development low normal Mental development below average Vineland SQ 91 "Child seclusive, suspicious, tense, uncommunicative, fearful, dependent"	WISC Full IQ 83 Verbal IQ 69 Performance IQ 103 D in reading; persistently withdrawn, shy, lacks self-confidence
0013-2 Female	Father farm laborer, first-grade education; mother fifth-grade education, works full-time in night shift in cannery while father takes care of child; mother rated "suggestible, contented, childlike, dull"; mother separated from husband for a while because of domestic problems	Physical development normal Cattell IQ 81 Vineland SQ 105 "Girl appears somewhat slow and dependent"	WISC Full IQ 83 Verbal IQ 74 Performance IQ 96 Fs in reading and arithmetic; Ds in grammar and spelling
1101-5 Female	Father utility man on farm, fourth-grade education; mother third-grade education; father has supplementary allowance from welfare; mother rated "mentally slow, suggestible"; continuous financial worries	Physical development normal Mental development low normal Cattell IQ 90 Vineland SQ 105	WISC Full IQ 82 Verbal IQ 74 Performance IQ 94 D in reading; distractible, shy; behavior reflects both physical and emotional deprivation
0260-1 Female	Head of household is laborer with sporadic employment record; conception occurred outside marriage while mother was separated from husband; financial troubles; mother hospitalized twice for psychotic episodes	Physical development normal Cattell IQ 87 Vineland SQ 104	WISC Full IQ 82 Verbal IQ 74 Performance IQ 85 Ds in reading, writing, and arithmetic; persistently

Case	Family background	Physical / developmental	Test results and behavior
	during pregnancy and postpartum period; rated "erratic, easygoing, careless, punitive, harsh"; both parents eighth-grade education		overaggressive, acts out problems
1505-2 Male	Father farm worker; mother ninth-grade education; child illegitimate; serious discord between parents for a long time before divorce, father had no time for child; mother became nervous and ill; lives with maternal grandmother and assorted relatives in old, messy house; mother rated "easygoing, dependent, careless, childlike"	Physical development normal Cattell IQ 83 Vineland SQ 91	WISC Full IQ 81 Verbal IQ 86 Performance IQ 79 Poor grades in reading, writing, and arithmetic; nervous, twitching, anxious, fidgety, distractible, restless
0401-1 Female	Mother 16 years old at time of pregnancy, comes from broken home; neither parent reads; father is laborer, unemployed most of the time and supported by welfare. Frequent domestic quarrels and separations. Mother rated "unintelligent, dependent, childlike, erratic"	No pediatric or psychological examinations at age two	WISC Full IQ 80 Verbal IQ 69 Performance IQ 97 Repeated first grade; Ds in reading, writing, and arithmetic; anxious, depressed, occasionally explosive behavior; truant from home
0891-3 Male	Father unskilled laborer; both parents eighth-grade education; mother rated "easygoing, careless, indifferent, lazy, unintelligent, childlike, suggestible, irresponsible"	Physical development normal Cattell IQ 79 Vineland SQ 104	WISC Full IQ 76 Stanford-Binet IQ 76 Asthma; obesity In class for educable mentally retarded; Ds in reading and arithmetic; Fs in spelling and grammer. Is unhappy, sulks; likes to be alone; angers easily

Code No.	Family Characteristics	Two-Year Status	10-Year Status
2223-1 Male	Father unemployed because of hypertension, depressed about his inability to support family; welfare assistance; father 10th-grade education, mother seventh-grade education; ill-kempt house with bare essentials; psychologist notes that child does not get appropriate stimulation at home	Physical development superior Cattell IQ 88 Vineland SQ 91	WISC Full IQ 70 Verbal IQ 67 Performance IQ 78 Obese Poor grades in reading, grammar, spelling, and arithmetic
1730-2 Female	Father laborer, has sixth-grade education; mother high school graduate; financial problems, but family reluctant to apply for public assistance because of "shame"; marginal living conditions; father appears mentally defective, fights with wife, beats children; mother rated "indifferent, ambivalent, child-like"	Physical development normal Cattell IQ 74 Vineland SQ 121	WISC Full IQ 70 Verbal IQ 82 Performance IQ 62 Repeated second grade; Fs in reading and arithmetic; Ds in grammar and spelling; perceptual problem
0184-1 Female	Father laborer, no formal education; mother eighth-grade education; family receives welfare assistance; 10 children always seem hungry; family lives in plantation camp where children play among selves only; two older sisters in special classes for mentally retarded children	Physical development normal Speech development slow	WISC Full IQ 70 Verbal IQ 70 Performance IQ 76 In class for educable mentally retarded; persistently withdrawn, shy, lacks self-confidence

178

Two and 10-Year Status of Children with Severe Perinatal Complications Who Grew Up in Homes Rated Low in Educational Stimulation and Emotional Support

Code No.	Perinatal Conditions	Family Characteristics	Two-Year Status	10-Year Status
2070-1 Male	Mother 31 hours labor; persistent OP [occipital-posterior presentation of head]; cesarean section; newborn cyanotic; oxygen administered; intermittent cyanosis; five days in incubator	Father semiskilled laborer; both parents eighth-grade education; mother worries about finances, husband's health (tuberculosis) and drinking; family supported by welfare	Physical development normal Cattell IQ 117 Vineland SQ 127 "Agreeable, deliberate, determined, eager, alert, responsive, quick"	PMA IQ 117 No school problems
2048-3 Female	Mother anemic; hospitalized for bleeding in second trimester; 37 hours labor; manual rotation; gestational age 34 weeks; weight 4 pounds 4 ounces; in incubator	Head of family is laborer; both parents eighth-grade education; mother not married to father of her child, rated "easily angered, punitive"	Physical development normal Cattell IQ 87 Vineland SQ 107 "Slow to relax, bashful, stubborn"	PMA IQ 112 Feelings hurt easily No school problems
0409-1 Male	Labor three hours; meconium staining; anoxia; continuous oxygen; in incubator; twitching of extremities at 18 hours	Father skilled laborer, works only part-time; family has some relief benefits; both parents seventh-grade education; mother worries about finances; older girls care for baby	Physical development normal Mental development normal	PMA IQ 105 Ds in reading, grammar, and spelling

Code No.	Perinatal Conditions	Family Characteristics	Two-Year Status	10-Year Status
1857-4 Female	Amnionitis; 70 hours labor; uterine inertia; forceps rotation; oxygen given to newborn	Father farm laborer; family has some welfare support; father no formal education; mother second grade; works in cannery during night shift; older children care for baby	Physical development low normal; seems under par Mental development normal	PMA IQ 103 No school problems
0801-1 Male	Eclampsia; mother hospitalized several times prepartum; postpartum convulsion	Father farm laborer, sixth-grade education; mother 10th-grade education; financial worries; husband not present most of the time	Physical development normal Mental development low normal	WISC Full IQ 102 Verbal IQ 97 Performance IQ 107 Repeated third grade; Ds in grammar, reading, spelling Emotional difficulties (hostility, resentment about home situation) interfering with school achievement
0495-1 Male	Forceps rotation; severe anoxia; cord compressed; first breath after seven minutes; resuscitation with oxygen and artificial respiration for 18 minutes; neck injured from forceps	Father farm laborer, first-grade education; mother fourth-grade education, hospitalized frequently with ulcers	Physical development normal Mental development normal	PMA IQ 99 Rheumatic fever Ds in reading, grammar, and spelling
1645-2	Mother mild diabetic;	Father laborer, has sev-	Physical development:	PMA IQ 99

180

Female	baby nine pounds; difficult delivery; low forceps; paralysis of upper extremities; tremors; baby kept in hospital for six weeks	enth-grade education; mother fourth-grade education	birth injury affecting right arm and shoulder; right shoulder somewhat spastic, weak right arm, slight right facial weakness; residual right Erb's palsy Mental development normal	Space 61 Perceptual 79 Bender-Gestalt errors 4 Slight hearing loss; residual Erb's palsy No school problems
0549-3 Female	Mother bleeding and threatened abortion in second trimester; placenta previa; emergency cesarean section; transfusion, delayed breath; resuscitation; tremors and apnea on second day; gestational age 30 weeks; weight 3 pounds 2 ounces; in incubator	Father farm laborer, no formal education; mother eighth-grade education; major family disorganization; family supported by welfare; maternal grandmother in control; mother very low in intelligence and maternal capacity	Physical development normal Mental development normal	WISC Full IQ 94 Verbal IQ 89 Performance IQ 101 Contact dermatitis Ds in reading, writing, arithmetic
1722-2 Female	Mother treated with X-rays for cancer of cervix; vaginal bleeding in third trimester; premature rupture of membrane (five days); cesarean section; newborn cry and respiration delayed; gestational age 29 weeks; weight 3 pounds 11 ounces	Father skilled laborer, has seventh-grade education; mother eighth-grade education; family discord; mother works in cannery part-time	Physical development low normal; probable anemia of prematurity Cattell IQ 89 Vineland SQ 95 "Slow to cooperate, bashful, hesitant, quiet; verbal limitation most marked"	PMA IQ 94 Ds in reading, writing, arithmetic

181

Code No.	Perinatal Conditions	Family Characteristics	Two-Year Status	10-Year Status
0319-3 Male	Mother severe pre-eclampsia, uterine inertia; induced labor; newborn severe jaundice; in incubator; gestational age 40 weeks; weight 4 pounds 12 ounces	Father farm laborer, fifth-grade education; mother ninth-grade education; welfare assistance; family discord; mother rated "careless, childlike, irresponsible, gives up easily"	Physical development normal Mental development normal	PMA IQ 92 Ds in reading, grammar, spelling
2103-2 Male	Mother pre-eclampsia; 3½ hours labor; newborn slow in breathing; feeble cry three minutes after delivery; oxygen administered; in incubator for one day; febrile sixth–eighth day; birth weight 4 pounds 7¾ ounces	Father unskilled laborer, often unemployed because of illness; family supported by welfare; father no formal education, mother seventh-grade education; parents worry about too many children and not enough money	Physical development normal Mental development normal	PMA IQ 91 Repeated first grade D in arithmetic
1894-2 Male	Mother very obese; prolonged labor; forceps rotation; gestational age 46 weeks; newborn anoxic; resuscitation needed; delayed cry and breathing	Father farm laborer; parents seventh-grade education; mother rated "careless, indifferent, easygoing, indulgent"	Physical development superior Cattell IQ 87 Vineland SQ 96 "Slightly questionable intellectual status; child inhibited, bashful, slow"	PMA IQ 87 No school problems
1876-2	Meconium-stained amni-	Father farm laborer,	Physical development:	WISC Full IQ 84

Male	otic fluid; cord around neck; newborn anoxic; first breath delayed seven minutes; poor color; mouth-to-mouth resuscitation and oxygen administration; in incubator; twitching right leg and left arm; turned cyanotic on second day; gestational age 39 weeks; weight 5 pounds 4 ounces	eighth-grade education; mother 11th-grade education, works night shift in cannery	right arm weak and uncoordinated; paralysis of right arm (cerebral palsy) Mental development normal	Verbal IQ 89 Performance IQ 82 Absence of proximal portion of radius, right arm Repeated second grade; problem in fine visual discrimination and motor coordination; daydreaming, marked inability to concentrate; chronic nervous habits
1622-1 Male	Mother had appendectomy in second trimester; 39 hours labor; LOP [left occipitalposterior presentation of head]; meconium staining; anoxia; three minutes until first cry and breathing	Mother illegitimate, unmarried, working fulltime to support child, rated "easily upset, tense, restless, discontented"	Physical development normal, except for undescended testis Mental development normal	WISC Full IQ 78 Verbal IQ 74 Performance IQ 87 Concern over lack of father and material things Ds in reading, writing, and arithmetic Daydreaming, immature
0958-1 Male	Placenta abruptio; profuse bleeding; prolapsed cord; breech extraction; double footling; anoxic, resuscitation with oxygen for three–four minutes; gestational age 37 weeks; weight 3 pounds 7 ounces; in incubator	Father skilled laborer, fourth-grade education; mother 11th-grade education; live with grandparents; mother had postpartum psychosis; family discord; mother rated "restless, demanding"	Physical development: head small Cattell IQ 74 Vineland SQ 96 "Bashful, fearful, hesitant, serious, slow"	PMA IQ 74 WISC Full IQ 77 Verbal IQ 75 Performance IQ 83 Bender-Gestalt errors 9 Attends class for educable mentally retarded; persistently aggressive, acts out problems

Code No.	Perinatal Conditions	Family Characteristics	Two-Year Status	10-Year Status
0231-4 Male	Amnionitis, infant poor color; premature rupture of membrane; double footling; oxygen in incubator; gestational age 35 weeks; weight 5 pounds ¾ ounce; oxygen by funnel on third day because of cyanosis; antibiotics; jaundice	Father farm laborer, seventh-grade education; mother ninth-grade education, works on the night shift in cannery	Physical development normal Mental development normal	WISC Full IQ 76 Verbal IQ 79 Performance IQ 78 Bender-Gestalt errors 8 Perceptual factor 68 Ds in reading, writing, arithmetic; perceptual problem
0151-2 Male	Mother bleeding for two days in third trimester; difficult delivery with forceps rotation; newborn cry delayed; oxygen resuscitation for five minutes	Head of family skilled laborer; family supported by welfare; mother appears retarded; neglects children; family discord; mother rated "restrictive, complaining, restless, impatient"	Physical development normal, except for umbilical hernia and depigmented dry red areas about lower trunk and legs; evidence of malnutrition Mental development normal	WISC IQ 75 Verbal IQ 79 Performance IQ 76 Hyperopic astigmatism; asthma After repeating first grade placed in class for educable mentally retarded; Ds in reading, writing, arithmetic; perceptual-motor problems; immature, distractible; chronic nervous habits
1698-2 Female	Mother hospitalized four times during pregnancy for threatened abortion; child is second twin, delivered 1 hour 15 minutes after first;	Father semiskilled laborer, has seventh-grade education; mother has fifth-grade education	Physical development: slightly dull-appearing, short, stocky infant; hospitalized seven times for convulsions and fever since nine months	WISC IQ 75 Verbal IQ 69 Performance IQ 86 Obesity In class for educable mentally retarded

ID	Birth / perinatal history	Family / social background	Development	Test results and school performance
	time of first breath delayed three minutes; cyanotic; oxygen administered; continued in incubator 34 hours; weight 4 pounds 7 ounces			
0055-4 Female	Mother severe preeclampsia; severe anemia; near shock at delivery; oxygen and blood transfusion; newborn cyanotic	Father laborer; mother fourth-grade education; family discord; baby given to senile and deaf grandmother for care; mother rated "childlike, irresponsible, unintelligent, erratic, indifferent, easygoing, careless"	Physical development low normal Cattell IQ 71 Vineland SQ 90 Child seems poorly cared for; "awkward, bashful, dependent, dull, fearful"	PMA IQ 69 Stanford-Binet IQ 64 Attends class for educable mentally retarded; Ds in reading, writing, arithmetic
0941-2 Male	Mother chronic nephritis and hypertension; diabetes, induced labor; newborn cry delayed; artificial respiration	Father laborer, often unemployed, is high school graduate; mother eighth-grade education, works part-time in pineapple cannery; mother separated from husband	Physical development normal Mental development normal; has "breath-holding" spells	WISC Full IQ 68 Verbal IQ 65 Performance IQ 78 Bender-Gestalt errors 7 Abnormal electroencephalogram (spiking in left temporal and parietal area); skull defect. Repeated first grade; Ds in reading and arithmetic; Fs in grammar and spelling; perceptual-motor problem; chronic nervous habits; hyperkinetic syndrome; restless, distractible

Code No.	Perinatal Conditions	Family Characteristics	Two-Year Status	10-Year Status
0635-1 Male	Breech extraction; double footling; resuscitation needed	Child illegitimate; mother 16 years old, married to man not father of child, skilled laborer; mother has 11th-grade education; rated "unintelligent, easygoing, childlike, suggestible, irresponsible"	Physical development: marked retardation; impression of cretinism Mental development: severe retardation Cattell IQ 30 Vineland SQ 20	Stanford-Binet IQ 39 Cretinism; hearing loss; divergent strabismus In training center for severely retarded children since seven years seven months of age
2129-1 Male	Mother cystitis; prolonged labor; newborn anoxic five minutes; artificial respiration required; weak, delayed cry; gestational age 32 weeks; weight 3 pounds 1 ounce; in incubator for one month	Father laborer, ninth-grade education; mother high school graduate, has worked outside home since baby was 11 months old; psychologist notes she is aware of child's slow development but not of implications; "gives up easily"	Physical development: microcephalus; spastic quadriplegia; questionable hearing Mental development: severe retardation Cattell IQ 20	Latest IQ below 30 Microcephaly; spastic quadriplegia; optic atrophy; epilepsy; hyperkinetic syndrome—restless, irritable, distractible In training center for severely retarded children

References

Abramowicz, M., and Kass, E. H. 1966. Pathogenesis and prognosis of prematurity. *New England Journal of Medicine* 275: 878–1059.

Anastasi, A. *Differential psychology*. 1958. New York: Macmillan.

Apgar, V.; Girdany, B. R.; McIntosh, R.; and Taylor, H. C., Jr. 1955. Neonatal anoxia. I. A study of the relation of oxygenation at birth to intellectual development. *Pediatrics* 15: 653–662.

Arenberg, D. L. 1960. The relations between delayed breathing at birth (apnea neonatorum) and subsequent intellectual, visual-motor, and motor development of children. Unpublished doctoral dissertation, Duke University.

Bayley, N. 1949. Consistency and variability in the growth of intelligence from birth to the eighteenth year. *Journal of Genetic Psychology* 75: 165–196.

———. 1954. Some increasing parent-child similarities during the growth of children. *Journal of Educational Psychology* 45: 1–21.

———. 1966. Developmental problems of the mentally retarded child. In *Prevention and treatment of mental retardation*, ed. I. Philips. New York: Basic Books.

Bayley, N., and Schaefer, E. 1964. Correlations of maternal and child behaviors with the development of mental abilities: Data from the Berkeley Growth Study. *Monographs of the Society for Research in Child Development*, serial 97, 29 (6).

Benaron, H.; Brown, M.; Tucker, B. E.; Wentz, V.; and Yacorzynski, G. K. 1953. The remote effect of prolonged labor with forceps delivery, precipitate labor with spontaneous delivery, and natural labor with spontaneous delivery on the child. *American Journal of Obstetrics and Gynecology* 66: 551–568.

Benaron, H.; Tucker, B. E.; Andrews, J. P.; Boshes, B.; Cohen, J.; Fromm, F.; and Yacorzynski, G. K. 1960. Effects of anoxia during labor and immediately after birth on the subsequent development of the child. *American Journal of Obstetrics and Gynecology* 80: 1129–1142.

Bernstein, B. 1960. Language and social class. *British Journal of Sociology* 11: 271–276.

Bierman, J. M.; Connor, A.; Vaage, M.; and Honzik, M. P. 1964. Pediatricians' assessment of intelligence of two year olds and their mental test scores. *Pediatrics* 34, 680–690.

Bierman, J. M., and French, F. 1963. Ecological influences on infant mortality among Japanese and Filipino immigrants to Hawaii. *Journal of Tropical Pediatrics and African Child Health* 9: 3–13.

Bierman, J. M.; Siegel, E.; French, F.; and Connor, A. 1963. The community impact of handicaps of prenatal or natal origin. *Public Health Reports* 78: 839–855.

Bierman, J. M.; Siegel, E.; French, F.; and Simonian, K. 1965. Analysis of the outcome of all pregnancies in a community. *American Journal of Obstetrics and Gynecology* 91: 37–45.

Bing, E. 1963. Effect of child-rearing practices on development of differential cognitive abilities. *Child Development* 34: 631–648.

Bloom, B. S. 1964. *Stability and change in human characteristics.* New York: Wiley.

Bolin, B. J. 1959. An investigation of the relationship between birth duration and childhood anxiety. *Journal of Mental Science* 105: 1045–1052.

Brambell, F. W. R. 1948. Prenatal mortality in mammals. *Biological Review* 23: 379–407.

Bronfenbrenner, U. 1958. Socialization and social class through time and space. In *Readings in Social Psychology*, eds. E. Maccoby, T. M. Newcomb, and E. L. Hartlett. New York: Holt, Rinehart & Winston.

Caldwell, B. 1964. The effects of infant care. In *Review of Child Development Research*, vol. 1, eds. M. Hoffman and W. Lois. New York: Russell Sage Foundation.

Campbell, W.; Cheseman, E.; and Kilpatrick, A. 1950. The effect of neonatal asphyxia on physical and mental development. *Archives of Diseases in Childhood* 25: 351–359.

Cattell, P. 1940. *The measurement of intelligence of infants.* New York: Psychological Corporation.

Caudill, W., and De Vos, G. 1956. Achievement, culture, and personality: The case of the Japanese-Americans. *American Anthropologist* 58: 1102–1126.

Cavanaugh, M. I.; Cohen, I.; Dunphy, D.; Ringwall, E. A.; and Goldberg, I. D. 1957. Prediction from the Cattell infant intelligence scale. *Journal of Consulting Psychology* 21: 33–37.

Chandrasekhar, S. 1959. *Infant mortality in India, 1901–1955.* London: G. Allen and Unwin.

Clifford, S. H. 1957. *Advances in pediatrics*, vol. 9. Chicago: Year Book Medical Publishers.

Corah, N. L.; Anthony, E. J.; Painter, P.; Sterm, J. A.; and Thurston, D. 1965. Effects of perinatal anoxia after seven years. *Psychological Monographs*, serial 596, 79 (3).

Crandall, V. J.; Dewey, R.; Katkovsky, W.; and Preston, A. 1964. Parents' attitudes and behaviors and grade-school children's academic achievements. *Journal of Genetic Psychology* 104: 53–66.

Darcy, N. T. 1953. A review of the literature on the effects of bilingualism upon the measurement of intelligence. *Journal of Genetic Psychology* 82: 21–57.

Darke, R. A. 1944. Late effect of severe asphyxia neonatorum. *Journal of Pediatrics* 24: 148–158.

Darsie, M. L. 1926. Mental capacity of American born Japanese children. *Comparative Psychology Monographs* 15 (3).

Dave, R. T. 1963. The identification and measurement of environmental process variables that are related to educational achievement. Unpublished doctoral dissertation, University of Chicago.

Doll, E. A. 1953. *Measurement of social competence.* Minneapolis: Educational Testing Bureau.

Douglas, J. W. B., and Bloomfield, J. M. 1958. *Children under five.* London: G. Allen and Unwin.

Drillien, C. M. 1964. *The growth and development of the prematurely born infant.* Baltimore: Williams & Wilkins.

Eisenberg, L. 1966. Reading retardation: 1. Psychiatric and sociologic aspects. *Pediatrics* 37: 352–363.

Ernhardt, C. L. 1952. Reporting of fetal deaths in New York City. *Public Health Reports* 67: 1161–1167.

Fraser, M. S., and Wilks, J. 1959. The residual effects of neonatal asphyxia. *Journal of Obstetrics and Gynecology of the British Commonwealth* 66: 748–752.

Frazer, J. F. D. 1955. Foetal death in the rat. *Journal of Embryology and Experimental Morphology* 3:13–29.

Freeberg, N., and Payne, D. 1967. Parental influence on cognitive development in early childhood: A review. *Child Development* 38: 66–87.

French, F., and Bierman, J. M. 1962. Probabilities of fetal mortality. *Public Health Reports* 77: 835–847.

French, F.; Connor, A.; Bierman, J. M.; Simonian, K.; and Smith, R. S. 1968. Congenital and acquired handicaps of 10 year olds: Report of a follow-up study, Kauai, Hawaii. *American Journal of Public Health* 58: 1388–1395.

French, F.; Howe, L. P.; Bierman, J. M.; Connor, A.; and Kemp, D. 1958. Communitywide pregnancy reporting in Kauai, Hawaii. *Public Health Reports* 73: 61–68.

Graham, F. K.; Caldwell, B. M.; Ernhart, C. B.; Pennoyer, M. M.; and Hartman, A. F. 1957. Anoxia as a significant perinatal experience: A critique. *Journal of Pediatrics* 50: 556–569.

Graham, F. K.; Ernhart, C. B.; Thurston, D.; and Craft, M. 1962. Development three years after perinatal anoxia and other potentially damaging newborn experiences. *Psychological Monographs*, serial 522, 76 (3).

Graham, F. K.; Pennoyer, M. M.; Caldwell, B. M.; Greenman, M.; and Hartman, A. F. 1957. Relationship between clinical status and behavior test performance in a newborn group with histories suggesting anoxia. *Journal of Pediatrics* 50: 177–189.

Gruenwald, Peter. 1965. Terminology of infants of low birth weight. *Developmental Medicine and Child Neurology* 7: 578–590.

Harrington, M. 1962. *The other America.* New York: Macmillan.

Havighurst, R. J., and Breese, F. F. 1947. Relation between ability and social status in a midwestern community. III: Primary mental abilities. *Journal of Educational Psychology* 38: 241–247.

Hawaii. 1959. *Statistical report of the Department of Health.* Honolulu.

Hertig, A. T.; Rock, J.; Adams, E. C.; and Menkin, M. C. 1959. Thirty-four fertilized human ova, good, bad and indifferent, recovered from women of known fertility: A study of biologic wastage in early human pregnancy. *Pediatrics* 23: 202–211.

Hess, R. D., and Shipman, V. C. 1965. Early experience and the socialization of cognitive modes in children. *Child Development* 36: 869–886.

Hindley, C. B. 1961. Social class influences on the development of ability in the first five years. In *Child and education: Proceedings of the XIV International Congress of Applied Psychology*, vol. 3., ed. G. Nielson, pp. 29–41. Copenhagen: Munksgaard.

Honzik, M. P. 1957. Developmental studies of parent-child resemblance in intelligence. *Child Development* 28: 215–228.

——. 1962. Mental and motor test performance of infants diagnosed or suspected of brain injury. Final report covering contract with National Institute of Neurological Diseases and Blindness, May 1962. Mimeographed. National Institutes of Health, U.S. Department of Health, Education, and Welfare.

——. 1963. A sex difference in the age of onset of the parent-child resemblance in intelligence. *Journal of Educational Psychology* 54: 231–237.

——. 1967. Environmental correlates of mental growth: Prediction from the family setting at 21 months. *Child Development* 38: 337–364.

Honzik, M. P.; Hutchings, J. J.; and Burnip, S. R. 1965. Birth record assessment and test performance at eight months. *American Journal of Diseases of Children* 109: 416–426.

Honzik, M. P.; Macfarlane, J.; and Allen, L. 1948. The stability of mental test performance between two and eighteen years. *Journal of Experimental Education* 17: 309–324.

Hueneman, R.; French, F.; and Bierman, J. M. 1961. Diets of pregnant women in Kauai, Hawaii. *Journal of the American Dietetic Association* 39: 569–577.

Hunt, J. M. 1961. *Intelligence and experience.* New York: Ronald Press.

Hytten, F. E., and Leitch, I. 1964. *The physiology of human pregnancy.* Oxford: Blackwell.

International Cooperation Administration. 1955. U.S. Operations Mission to the Philippines, Health and Sanitation Division annual report for 1955.

Irwin, O. 1960. Infant speech: Effect of systematic reading of stories. *Journal of Speech and Hearing Research* 3: 187–190.

Japan. 1960. Ministry of Health and Welfare. Statistics relating to maternal and child health.

Jones, H. E., and Bayley, N. 1941. The Berkeley Growth Study. *Child Development* 12: 167–173.

Kagan, J. 1964. American longitudinal research. *Child Development* 35: 1–32.

Kagan, J., and Freeman, M. 1963. Relation of childhood intelligence, maternal behaviors, and social class to behavior during adolescence. *Child Development* 34: 899–911.

Kagan, J., and Moss, H. A. 1959. Parental correlates of child's IQ and height: A cross-validation of the Berkeley Growth Study results. *Child Development* 30: 325–332.

——. 1962. *Birth to maturity: A study in psychological development.* New York: Wiley.

Keith, H. M., and Gage, R. P. 1960. Neurologic lesions in relation to asphyxia of the newborn and factors of pregnancy: Long-term follow-up. *Pediatrics* 26: 616–622.

Keith, H. M.; Norval, M. A.; and Hunt, A. B. 1953. Neurologic lesions in relation to the sequelae of birth injury. *Neurology* 3: 139–147.

Kent, N., and Davis, D. R. 1957. Discipline in the home and intellectual development. *British Journal of Medical Psychology* 30: 27–34.

Kitano, H. 1961. Different child-rearing attitudes between first and second generation Japanese in the United States. *Journal of Social Psychology* 53: 13–19.

Knobloch, H., and Pasamanick, B. 1959. The syndrome of minimal brain damage in infancy. *Journal of the American Medical Association* 70: 1384–1387.

———. 1960. An evaluation of the consistency and predictive value of the forty week Gesell Developmental Schedule. *Psychiatric Research Reports* 13: 10–31.

———. 1966. Prediction from the assessment of neuro-motor and intellectual status in infancy. Paper presented at the American Psycho-pathological Association Meeting, 18–20 February 1966.

Kogan, J., and Freeman, M. 1963. Relation of childhood intelligence, maternal behavior and social class to behavior during adolescence. *Child Development* 34: 899–911.

Koppitz, E. 1964. *The Bender-Gestalt test for young children.* New York: Grune & Stratton.

Lancet no. 7450. 1966. Annotations: Small for dates. 1: 1309–1310.

Lee, R. K. 1954. Public health contrasts in Hawaii, 1850–1953. *Public Health Reports* 69: 403–409.

Lesser, G. S.; Fifer, G. M.; and Clark, D. H. 1965. Mental abilities of children from different social class and cultural groups. *Monographs of the Society for Research in Child Development,* serial 102, 30 (4).

Lind, A. W. 1946. *Hawaii's Japanese.* Princeton: Princeton University Press.

———. 1955. *Hawaii's people.* 1st ed. Honolulu: University of Hawaii Press.

———. 1967. *Hawaii's people.* 3rd ed. Honolulu: University of Hawaii Press.

McCandless, B. R. 1965. Environment and intellectual functioning. In *Mental retardation,* eds. H. Stevens and R. Heber, pp. 175–209. Chicago: University of Chicago Press.

Maccoby, E. E., ed. 1966. *The development of sex differences.* Stanford: Stanford University Press.

Macfarlane, J. W. 1938. Studies in child guidance: I. Methodology of data collection and organization. *Monographs of the Society for Research in Child Development,* serial 19, 3 (6).

McGrade, B. J.; Kessen, W.; and Leutzendorff, A. 1965. Activity in the human newborn as related to delivery difficulty. *Child Development* 36: 73–79.

MacKinney, L. G. 1958. Asphyxia neonatorum in relation to mental retardation: Current studies in man. In *Neurological and psychological deficits of asphyxia neonatorum,* ed. W. F. Windle, pp. 195–218. Springfield, Ill.: Charles C. Thomas.

McPhail, F. L., and Hall, E. L. 1941. Consideration of cause and possible later effect of anoxia in the newborn infant. *American Journal of Obstetrics and Gynecology* 42: 686–701.

Miller, A.; Margolin, J.; and Yolles, S. 1957. Epidemiology of reading disabilities: Some methodological considerations and early findings. *American Journal of Public Health* 47: 1250–1256.

Miller, F. J. W.; Court, S. D. M.; Walton, W. S.; and Knox, E. G. 1960. *Growing up in Newcastle upon Tyne.* London: Oxford University Press.

Milner, E. A. 1951. A study of the relationship between reading readiness in grade one school children and patterns of parent-child interaction. *Child Development* 22: 95–112.

Moore, T. 1968. Language and intelligence: A longitudinal study of the first eight years. Part II: Environmental correlates of mental growth. *Human Development* 11: 1–24.

Niswander, K. R.; Turoff, B. B.; and Romans, J. 1966. Developmental status of children delivered through elective induction. *Obstetrics and Gynecology* 27: 15–20.

Norbeck, E. 1959. *Pineappletown: Hawaii.* Berkeley: University of California Press.

Norbeck, E., and De Vos, G. 1960. Japan. In *Psychological Anthropology,* ed. F. Hsu. Homewood, Ill.: Dorsey Press.

North, A. F. 1966. Small-for-dates neonates: Maternal, gestational and neonatal characteristics. *Pediatrics* 38: 1013–1019.

Nydegger, W. F., and Nydegger, C. 1963. Tarong: An Ilocos barrio in the Philippines. In *Six cultures: Studies of childrearing,* ed. B. Whiting. New York: Wiley.

Oppenheimer, S., and Kessler, J. W. 1963. Mental testing of children under 3 years. *Pediatrics* 31: 865.

Pasamanick, B., and Knobloch, H. 1960. Brain damage and reproductive casualty. *American Journal of Orthopsychiatry* 30: 298–305.

Perinatal Research Branch, National Institute of Neurological Diseases and Blindness, National Institutes of Health. Annual Reports on the Collaborative Study of Cerebral Palsy and Other Childhood Disorders, 1960–present. Washington, D.C. U.S. Department of Health, Education, and Welfare, Public Health Service.

Perry, J. S. 1954. Fecundity and embryonic mortality in pigs. *Journal of Embryology and Experimental Morphology* 2: 308–322.

Philippines. 1921. Census of the Philippine Islands: Population and mortality. II Census Office, Manila, Philippines.

Philippines. 1946. Yearbook of statistics, pp. 205–210.

Porteus, S. D. 1965. *The Porteus Maze Test: Fifty years of application.* Palo Alto: Pacific Book Publishers.

Prechtl, H. F. R. 1960. The long term value of the neurological examination of the newborn infant. In *Child neurology and cerebral palsy. Little club clinics in developmental medicine,* no. 2, p. 69. London: Medical Advisory Committee of the National Spastics Society.

———. 1965. Prognostic value of neurological signs in the newborn infant. *Proceedings of the Royal Society of Medicine* 58: 3.

Qulligan, E. S. 1968. Tracing the damage. *In* His right to be normal, by C. Valenti. *Saturday Review* 51 (Dec. 7, 1968): 77.

Roberts, S. O., and Robinson, J. M. 1952. Intercorrelations of the Primary Mental Abilities Test for 10 year olds by socioeconomic status, sex and race. *American Psychologist* 7: 304–305.

Schachter, F. F., and Apgar, V. 1959. Perinatal asphyxia and psychologic signs of brain damage in childhood. *Pediatrics* 24: 1016–1025.

Schachter, M. 1950. Observations on the prognosis of children born following trauma at birth. *American Journal of Mental Deficiency* 54: 456–463.

Shapiro, S., and Moriyama, I. M. 1963. International trends in infant mortality and their implications for the United States. *American Journal of Public Health* 53: 747–760.

Sikkema, M. 1947. Observations on Japanese early child training. *Psychiatry* 10: 423–430.

Skeels, H. M. 1966. Adult status of children with contrasting early life experiences. *Monographs of the Society for Research in Child Development*, serial 105, 31 (3).

Skodak, M., and Skeels, H. M. 1949. A final follow-up study of one hundred adopted children. *Journal of Genetic Psychology* 75: 85–125.

Smith, C., and Keogh, B. 1962. The group Bender-Gestalt test as a reading readiness screening instrument. *Perceptual and Motor Skills* 15: 639–645.

Sontag, L. W.; Baker, C. T.; and Nelson, B. L. 1958. Mental growth and personality development: A longitudinal study. *Monographs of the Society for Research in Child Development*, serial 68, 23 (2).

Spence, J.; Walton, W. S.; Miller, F. J. W.; and Court, S. D. M. 1954. *A thousand families in Newcastle upon Tyne*. London: Oxford University Press.

Stechler, G. 1964. A longitudinal follow-up of neonatal apnea. *Child Development* 35: 333–348.

Stevenson, S. S. 1948. Parental factors affecting adjustment in childhood. *Pediatrics* 2: 154–162.

Strong, E. 1934. *The second generation Japanese problem*. Palo Alto: Stanford University Press.

Taylor, W. F. 1964. On the methodology of measuring the probability of fetal death in a prospective study. *Human Biology* 36: 86–103.

Teuber, H., and Rudel, R. G. 1962. Behavior after cerebral lesions in children and adults. *Developmental Medicine and Child Neurology* 4: 3–20.

Thomson, A. M., and Billewicz, W. Z. 1963. Nutritional status, maternal physique and reproductive efficiency. *Proceedings Nutrition Society* 22: 55.

Thurstone, L., and Thurstone, T. G. 1954. *SRA primary mental abilities, examiner manual*. Chicago: Science Research Associates.

Ucko, L. E. 1965. A comparative study of asphyxiated and non-asphyxiated boys from birth to five years. *Developmental Medicine and Child Neurology* 7: 643–657.

United Nations. 1960. *Demographic yearbook*. New York: United Nations.

United Nations. 1961. *Demographic yearbook*. New York: United Nations.

U.S. Dept. of Commerce. Bureau of the Census. 1963. *1960 census of housing*, vol. 1. *States and small areas*. Washington, D.C.

U.S. Dept. of Health, Education, and Welfare. National Center for Health Statistics, Vital Statistics Division. 1962. Study group on development of recommendations for evaluation, improvement, and utilization of data on congenital malformations from vital records, document 53112. Offset. Washington, D.C.

Usdin, G. L., and Weil, M. L. 1952. Effect of apnea neonatorum on intellectual development. *Pediatrics* 9: 387–394.

Walters, R. H. 1958. The intelligence test performance of Maori children: A cross-cultural study. *Journal of Abnormal and Social Psychology* 57: 107–114.

Wechsler, D. 1949. *Wechsler intelligence scale for children*. New York: Psychological Corporation.

Weickart, D. P. 1967. Preschool programs: Preliminary findings. *Journal of Special Education* 1: 163–182.

Werner, E. 1969. Sex differences in correlations between children's IQ's and measures of parental ability and environmental ratings. *Developmental Psychology* 1: 3.

Werner, E.; Bierman, J. M.; French, F.; Simonian, K.; Connor, A.; Smith, R. S.; and Campbell, M. 1968. Reproductive and environmental casualties: A report on the 10 year follow-up of the children of the Kauai pregnancy study. *Pediatrics* 42: 112–127.

Werner, E.; Honzik, M. P.; and Smith, R. S. 1968. Prediction of intelligence and achievement at 10 years from 20 months pediatric and psychologic examinations. *Child Development* 39: 4, 1063–1075.

Werner, E., and Simonian, K. 1966. The social maturity of preschool children in Hawaii: Results of a community–wide survey and a review of two decades of research. *Journal of Social Psychology* 69: 197–207.

Werner, E,; Simonian, K.; Bierman, J. M.; and French, F. 1967. Cumulative effect of perinatal complications and deprived environment on physical, intellectual, and social development of preschool children. *Pediatrics* 39: 490–505.

Werner, E.; Simonian, K.; and Smith, R. S. 1967. Reading achievement, language functioning, and perceptual-motor development of 10 and 11 year olds. *Perceptual and Motor Skills* 25: 409–420.

——. 1968. Ethnic and socioeconomic status differences in abilities and achievement among preschool and school-age children in Hawaii. *Journal of Social Psychology* 75: 43–59.

Whiting, B., ed. 1963. *Six cultures: Studies of child-rearing.* New York: Wiley.

Wolf, R. M. 1964. The identification and measurement of environmental process variables related to intelligence. Unpublished doctoral dissertation, University of Chicago.

——. 1965. The measurement of environment. Paper presented at the Invitational Conference on Testing Problems, Princeton, New Jersey, 1965.

World Health Organization. 1961. Public health aspects of low birth weight. Technical Report Series 217.

Wortis, H.; Bardach, J. L.; Cutler, R.; Rue, R.; and Freedman, A. 1963. Child rearing practices in a low socioeconomic group. *Pediatrics* 32: 298–307.

Yarrow, L. 1963. Research in dimensions of early maternal care. *Merrill-Palmer Quarterly* 9: 101–114.

Yerushalmy, J.; Berg, B. J. van den; Erhardt, C. L.; and Jacobziner, H. 1965. Birth weight and gestation as indices of "immaturity." *American Journal of Diseases of Children* 109: 43–57.

Yerushalmy, J.; Bierman, J. M.; Kemp, D.; Connor, A.; and French, F. 1956. Longitudinal studies of pregnancy on the island of Kauai. *American Journal of Obstetrics and Gynecology* 71: 80–96.

Index

Achievement problems, 135–136; prediction of, 96–97, 99–101; relationship of socioeconomic status to, 69
Age of mother, related to perinatal complications, 39
Amyotonia congenita, at birth, 44
Anemia, hemolytic: at age 10, 63, 95, 96
Anglo-Caucasian children: educational stimulation given in the home, 118, 120; emotional support given in the home, 118; no language problems, 116; percentage with behavioral problems, 117; percentage with perceptual problems, 117; percentage with school achievement problems, 113; ratings on Cattell Infant Intelligence Test, 112, 135–136; ratings on Science Research Associates Primary Mental Abilities Test, 117–118, 135–136; ratings on Vineland Social Maturity Scale, 111–112; skin defects at birth, 44
Anglo-Caucasians: fertility rate of, 111; immigration to Kauai of, 10; jobs held by, 103; percentage bearing infants of low birth weights, 36–37; percentage of live births in 1955, 103; social mobility of, 10
Anus, imperforate: at birth, 44
Asthma, severe: at age 10, 63, 95
Auditory atresia: at age 10, 22, 63; at age two, 94

Bayley Mental and Motor Scales, 53
Behavior: of child, correlated with perinatal stress, 7, 52, 67; of mother, correlated with intelligence of child, 59–60; problems of, 63, 131, 134
Bender-Gestalt Test, 63, 67, 101; results of group, 19, 21; results of individual, 21, 84; use of, to measure perceptual problems, 117
Beriberi, 108

Berkeley Growth Study, 3, 5, 58, 124
Berkeley Guidance Study, 58, 59, 125, 129
Biliary atresia, at birth, 44
Birth rate: by national origin, 11; in 1955, 12
Blindness, 63, 94
Brain injuries at birth: effect on behavior, 5

California Test of Mental Maturity, use of, to measure parental ability, 28
Cattell Infant Intelligence Scale, 17, 48, 49, 53, 55, 77–91 passim, 100, 101, 121, 125, 134, 135–136; use of, in comparing ethnic groups, 112–113; use of, to predict school achievement problems at 10 years, 99
Caucasians. *See* Anglo-Caucasians. *See also* Portuguese; Spanish
Census, preliminary, 14, 24
Central nervous system, defects of: at age 10, 22, 63, 134
Cerebral palsy: at age 10, 22, 63, 67; at age two, 94; at birth, 41
Child Training and Rehabilitation Center, 13
Chinese: immigration to Kauai of, 9; social mobility of, 10
Cleft lip and palate: at age 10, 22, 63; at age two, 94; at birth, 44
Complications, perinatal: system of scoring, 15–16
Conceptual abilities, as affected by perinatal stress, 5
Congenital defects: early recognition of, in study, 44–45; at two years, 46
Cretinism, 67, 78
Crippled Children's Branch of the Children's Health Services Division, 16–17, 44–45, 94; as source of information, 19

195